Globalization from the Bottom Up

A. Coskun Samli

Globalization from the Bottom Up

A Blueprint for Modern Capitalism

 Springer

A. Coskun Samli
University of North Florida
Jacksonville, FL
USA
jsamli@unf.edu

ISBN: 978-0-387-77097-0   e-ISBN: 978-0-387-77098-7
DOI: 10.1007/978-0-387-77098-7

Library of Congress Control Number: 2008923326

9 8 7 6 5 4 3 2 1

springer.com

This book is dedicated to the ambitious twenty-first-century capitalists who understand the importance of building a better world.

A.C.S

Preface

The net profit of Exxon for the year 2005 was reported to be almost $8 billion which reflected about 40 percent growth in its profit picture within a year. As profit pictures of fuel, arms, medical services and financial services industries among others reach unbelievable levels, by definition, most consumers get poorer because they have less money left for other essentials for their lives such as food, education, medical needs, and housing. Adding insult to injury, of the 100 largest budgets in the world, 52 belong to private corporations. Needless to say, such accumulation of economic power and such mind-boggling profit pictures do not encourage any movement on the part of these powerhouse companies to reach out and do something about the troubled world within which they have amassed such economic and indeed indirectly political power. This is a questionable view of the world; I have to get more power before others do it and I get it at the expense of others. This is what this author coins the GREED FACTOR. As has been said, power corrupts and absolute power corrupts absolutely. The greed factor unfortunately is at the threshold of absolute power that corrupts absolutely. Unchecked and unguided continuity of this orientation is bound to bring disaster to this very fragile planet called the earth. We must establish a point of view that if the world we live in does better, there will be more for everyone. In other words, everyone will be better off economically. This is the ambition that power structures in the world must use instead of being corrupted by absolute power. *Greed versus ambition*, this is the basic theme of this book.

Webster (1968) defines capitalism as "the economic system in which all or most of the means of production and distribution owned and operated for profit originally under fully competitive conditions; it has been generally characterized by a tendency toward concentration of wealth and in its later phase by the growth of great corporations" (*Webster's New Twentieth Century Dictionary*, New York: The Word Publishing Company, 269).

The same dictionary defines laissez faire as the people do as they please.

These two concepts today, as they did in the 18th century, control the real power in the world and can be easily pointed out as the cause of all of the ills of the world and also as the solution of all of the ills of the world. Whereas capitalism and a tendency toward creating a laissez-faire atmosphere in the 18th and 19th centuries at least created competition, and those competitors appeared to be ambitious enough to create wealth for societies as they create wealth for themselves. This picture, in time, reversed itself. By the 21st century, the emergence of global corporate giants has accumulated much economic and political power through the capital they generated and have become more inclined to bypass competition by mergers, by acquisitions, and by putting much pressure on governments to become smaller and to deregulate. They have been engaged in bid-rigging, price fixing, improper accounting, and other activities, all of which create no value for the consumers and the society. Thus, traditional capitalism has become more greed-driven than ambition-driven as 18th- and 19th-century competition gave way to business size and commensurate economic power. Particularly in the second half of the 20th century, many greed-driven global corporate giants by accumulating economic power through mergers and acquisitions became instrumental in accelerated globalization movement which is described as Darwinism on steroids (Friedman 2000, Samli 2004). Although globalization can be and in some cases is a tremendous power, in its present form, it is mostly creating a critically separated a few extremely rich and many extremely poor people all over the world. This is based on the movement from ambition to greed. At the writing of this book, most American airlines are driving themselves into bankruptcy not because their flights are empty, on the contrary they are totally full, but a Chapter 11 status will enable them to do away with most of the retirement and medical burdens. They will create hundreds of thousands of retired employees almost totally poor. That is greed. It will make a few extremely rich as it will create widespread misery.

In the 18th and 19th centuries, although much accumulation of economic power occurred, this was the outcome of capitalism and laissez faire working together and rewarding ambition and hard work. During that era, there were also much competition and eventually laws against accumulating too much economic power. Legal conditions and encouraged competition did not allow the ambition factor to go in the direction of the greed factor. But in the 20th century, particularly the last 25 years of it, capitalism changed its nature and moved away from ambition into *greed*. As economic power accumulated in the hands of a few through mergers and acquisitions, the laws against accumulating too much economic power became powerless. During the last quarter of the 20th century, this greed factor combined with high tech and globalization became almost a danger to the future of this fragile planet called earth. The frightening global expansion of high tech-based economic power has created *underclasses* in most parts of the world (Glassman 2000, Isaak 2005). As the underclasses emerge, more and more economic power accumulates in the hands of the few superrich. Here the temptation to move from ambition to greed becomes obvious. Thus, the modern capitalists should not be left totally alone unchecked with perfect or near-perfect laissez-faire conditions, where the winner takes all. Perhaps because of human frailty or perhaps because absolute power corrupts absolutely, there will be no limit to amassing economic wealth by a few as the rest of many societies struggle to survive. Telling people you are on your own but be fair is telling the rich to live like the poor will not happen. Instead, the rich and the powerful have been pushing for more and more privatization which will give them a greater power to exercise greed. But seeing the grave danger in how globalization is speeding up the ability to amass more economic wealth and how it is magnifying the chasm between the rich and the poor is the necessary first step. This must be seen not as an act of necessary altruistic outreach but a necessity for survival if the world were to have a future.

The movement from ambition to greed can change (and is changing) the general structure and the profile of the whole world in a questionable manner. As haves become have-mores, have-nots are becoming have-nothings, the gap between the rich and the poor widens. As the poor of the world live in disease, deprivation, and hopelessness, it is very difficult to think of a world that is hostility and terrorism free. In the meantime, the physical qualities of this fragile planet are also deteriorating. This deterioration is also mainly attributed to the greed factor inculcated by lack of compassion and understanding. This author believes that the global laissez fairism, as it stands, is in a self destructive mode and globalization as it is practiced presently cannot be sustained. Thus, this book deals with capitalism with some modified laissez-faire orientation which is coined here as *social capitalism*. While laissez-faire capitalism is causing many problems and threatening the future of the world, social capitalism can be a major solution for all of the world's problems.

It Is Not Adam Smith or Karl Marx

In the 18th century, Adam Smith presented his economic philosophy in his famous book, *The Wealth of Nations*. Subsequently at the beginning of the 19th century, Karl Marx articulated his economic stance in his famous book, *Das Capital*. In terms of Hegelian dialectic, it can be posited that Smith's work is the *thesis* and Marx's work is the *antithesis*. For centuries, laissez-faire capitalists have been fighting off Marxist communists and vice-versa. One may say in the name of true Hegelian orientation the *synthesis* is missing. Capitalists in the last part of the 20th century have proved their greater resilience than communists. However, in its somewhat exaggerated and unchallenged ways, modern capitalism is not going quite in the direction that would be totally beneficial to the whole world. In a sense, the present author puts forth this book as a synthesis of Smith's and Marx's works. It is hoped that it makes a major positive impact toward improving the economic picture of the world.

Samli (2004) pointed out that a large proportion of the world's population is passed over during the current globalization process. He further pointed out that this forgotten majority represents a big market which promises to be profitable for those who can enter this market successfully. Prahalad (2005) in a remarkable book points out that the world's population can be categorized in the form of a pyramid with five tiers. Just as Samli, he points out that about one-third of the world's population is placed at the bottom of the global economic pyramid which is composed of these five tiers. It is reiterated by this author that there is much market power in the lower levels of this pyramid. If modern capitalism modifies its approach of catering only to the top two tiers and pays more attention to these emerging world markets which are the bottom three tiers of the world's economic pyramid, much consumer value will be generated and many profitable transactions will take place. The concerned and compassionate capitalists of the world, thus, could make much money as they narrow the gap between the rich and the poor.

Could Capitalism Make a Contribution?

In essence, this book is about 21st-century capitalism, not the way it is but the way it should be. First, it presents the point of view that if the markets within which capitalism functions and prospers do not survive, capitalism fails also. Thus capitalism must make a contribution to the well-being of the market system. Second, the proposed 21st-century capitalism must comprehend that survival of markets and capitalism is intimately interrelated. The two must surge forward together. However, globalization which is a very powerful and broad expansion of 21st-century greed-driven capitalism is not considered sustainable by many international thinkers (Samli 2002). In other words, the current version of capitalism in its global undertakings is not simultaneously feeding the markets within which it is functioning. The author maintains that 21st-century capitalism must establish certain levels of self-discipline and must become sustainable if we expect a future for the world. More toned down and balanced capitalism that is reaching to remote markets of the emerging countries and generating enough wealth to bridge the gap between haves and have-nots must be considered not only but also extremely necessary for the future of the fragile planet.

Throughout this book, I am asserting that capitalism, global or national, is not an end only but a very powerful means to an end; but in order to reach a meaningful end, there must be changes in the thinking and the orientation of modern capitalists. I further assert that without a proper balance of public and private sectors involvement in modern capitalism, global poverty cannot be alleviated and global potential benefits of capitalism cannot materialize. The goal of a modified global capitalism has to be reasonable and sustainable prosperity, not for a few lucky, select capitalists, but for all. Prahalad (2005) asserts the need for dignity and choice for those who are at the bottom of the emerging countries are very critical for global capitalism. This is a critical progression over the current status of the world economies. Without such progress, we face a very bleak future. However, I also maintain that dignity and choice can be achieved only if some modification and practices in modern capitalism take place. It is possible to generate the implied dignity and choice through market systems and also achieve satisfactory profits as well. But there must be some conscientious effort in that direction.

A Social Evolution

Medawar as early as 1959 raised a very important question, asking whether man is potentially capable of further evolution or whether evolution has reached its absolute limits. It is difficult to answer this question in biological terms; however, in social and economic terms, there is much room for evolutionary or indeed for revolutionary change and progress. The most frustrating aspect of the current picture that can be drawn from the existing status of the world is that we know more what can and should happen as things get worse but we (the global majority, the majority of thinking people or the majority of those who are in power) are not doing enough to reverse the progressively deteriorating situations so that the fragile planet called earth will be a good home for many generations yet to come. The present author believes that the planet is in a self-destructive mode. If John F. Kennedy were alive today, he might have revised his famous statement: "My fellow Americans, ask not what your country can do for you, ask what you can do for your country" to "My fellow citizens of the world, ask not what this fragile planet could do for you, ask what you can do for it." In another remarkable book, Hertz (2001) maintains that global capitalism is silently taking over and killing democracy. In other words, global capitalism in its present form is not quite fair, in fact it is not even democratic. Just why might the present author, who is a marketing specialist, be engaged in an undertaking of this magnitude? A very important topic such as building a better world appears to be a monumental task, so why would anybody tackle such a challenge? Well, basically we in the marketing discipline undertake research, thinking and writing in the areas of generating consumer value, not just for a few select or privileged consumers, but for all consumers throughout the world. Therefore, I believe that my point of view throughout this book is practical and application oriented. Furthermore, I think that unless we thinkers and doers of economic activity take a holistic approach to the world's problems, there can be no progress. In other words, the all-encompassing macroproblems of the world cannot be micromanaged. It is reiterated numerous times in this book that the world's economy is like a ship, if there is a high tide (or general economic progress), everybody in the ship benefits, in that economic conditions improve for all. But if there is a low tide, on the other hand (deterioration of economic conditions for the poor or the forgotten majority), everyone loses. It is critical to explore how an economic high tide can be reached and maintained. Instead, much of the literature deals with how to establish global dominance (Hertz 2001). To put it differently, global dominance deals with how to reach the top layer of this ship and benefit only those who are there, regardless of the tide. But it must be understood that if the ship experiences a very low tide and hits the bottom of the sea and capsizes, then those who are on the upper deck also face as much risk as those on the lower deck. To reach a high tide, the people in the lower deck must be taken care of. They have needs to be satisfied and although limited have some income to pay for the goods and services to satisfy these needs. These conditions present tremendous profit potential and lift the global ship to a higher economic tide.

Instead of dealing with many personalized examples of desperate conditions of different individuals, the author believes in making an analysis of the most critical threats to the world's well-being and different ways of coping with these. Toward the end of the book, I start making some very important recommendations so that the fragile planet can be saved and its dwellers can enhance their quality of life as providers of goods and services make money also. In other words, modern capitalism can remedy the ills of the fragile planet and can create profits in doing so.

The author believes that every region, every organization, and every company that is greedily micromanaged or micromismanaged without paying much attention to the macroenvironment, is taking a shortcut to destruction. Establishing environmental responsibilities, coordinating these responsibilities, taking advantage of magnificent powers of globalization, and making sure that brute power will neither accumulate nor be used in the form of a zero-sum game are broader dimensions of what this book is all about.

It is posited here that examining the all-encompassing macroissues and finding alternative macrosolutions to macroproblems makes a major and powerful contribution to microconditions as well. However, being exclusively involved with microissues is not necessarily beneficial to the macroproblems of the fragile planet. Acknowledging that earth is a fragile planet threatened by population explosion, depletion of resources, all kinds of pollution, poverty, and, above all, by the greed factor of 21st-century capitalism could secure a safer and more prosperous future for all, bar none. Acknowledging these problems, hopefully, will yield practical and positive solutions for the whole world. And such solutions would benefit all inhabitants of the fragile planet.

About this Book

This book, in general, indicates that micromanagement of macroproblems is endangering the future of the fragile planet. Just blind profiteering without paying attention to the overall health of markets is not sustainable. There are 13 chapters in the book.

Chapter 1 explores the broad current problems of the world. It points out that the gap between the rich and the poor has reached new heights. Middle classes are slowly disappearing. Insecurities are increasing and are leading to clashes of civilizations. Much of these are created by the greed factor.

Chapter 2 presents the position that as economic gaps widen and global hostilities are becoming more pronounced, lines of demarcation are drawn. This situation is leading to more militaristic behavior patterns. Lack of education is fueling this situation.

Chapter 3 discusses the environmental problems of the fragile planet. Depleting natural resources, unchecked population explosion, disappearing forests, air and water pollution, and global warming are among the most critical issues.

Chapter 4 examines the current status of globalization. Although a critical tool for overall improvement, the current pattern of globalization is considered not sustainable.

Chapter 5 recapitulates on how wealth is generated in societies. Understanding this all-important topic makes it easier to find solutions for the world's problems.

Chapter 6 presents a different orientation to globalization. Instead of top-down globalization, which may be considered a continuation of imperialism, a bottom-up globalization that will take care of the forgotten majority of the world's consumers is proposed.

Chapter 7 indicates that entrepreneurship is the key factor that can create a bottom-up globalization. A culture of entrepreneurship can facilitate the emergence of this whole process. Similarly, it proposes a facsimile of a Silicon Valley for every country in an effort to develop their economies through more endogenous efforts.

Chapter 8 presents a number of possible solutions to the enormous problems that the fragile planet is experiencing. It is further posited in this chapter that international entrepreneurial partnering can play an extremely valuable role.

Chapter 9 advocates economic progress for all, not only for a few select parties. It points out that the world economy is not a zero-sum game and should not be treated as such.

Chapter 10 maintains that the lower tiers of the global economic pyramid require more consumer protection than the upper tiers.

Chapter 11 puts forth some of the general characteristics of a global ethical code. Without such a code in practice *the wolves will always eat the sheep*.

Chapter 12 explores the future. It reiterates the key problems of the fragile planet and advocates the necessity of a blueprint that is helpful in coordinating global efforts to solve the problems. It points out that macroproblems cannot be resolved through micromanagement. Above all, this chapter presents a point of view of how the modified and improved capitalism of the 21st century can be implemented.

Chapter 13 deals with financing the future of a better world. It points out that globalization stimulated by social capitalism must be financed in less conventional procedures. It also reinforces the importance of endogenous growth.

Finally, a Postscript attempts to put together a proactive agenda that can help build a better world by creating global riches.

Acknowledgments

A book such as this one cannot be completed without the help of many people. Research assistants Tomas Miho, Jennifer Howard, and Merici Fevrier were extremely helpful. The author benefited from discussing cases and events with people such as Professor Adel El-Ansary, Ronald Adams, and Fred Pragasam of the University of North Florida. My students were subjected to many ideas that are in the book. They reacted favorably or unfavorably, and the author took notice. My friends overseas and in different parts of the country; Osman Samli, my brother in Turkey, Professor Joseph M. Sirgy of Virginia Tech, and Dean Edward M. Mazze of the University of Rhode Island were contacted on and off. Beverly Chapman lent her editorial skills to the author and, as usual, she did a great job. The department head at the University of North Florida, Huel E. Baker III, gave the author much needed support, and our secretaries Leanna Payne, Michelle Green, and Carolyn Gavin pitched in to type the manuscript from barely legible handwritten notes. Nick Philipson, Senior Editor, was extremely helpful in making suggestions and interacting with the author. To these and many other people who influenced my thinking, I am grateful. However, I hasten to add that the ideas that are presented and positions that are taken throughout this book are my own, and I am solely responsible for them.

References

Friedman, Thomas L. (2000), *The Lexus and The Olive Tree*, New York: Achor Books.

Glassman, Ronald M. (2000), *Caring Capitalism*, New York: St. Martin's Press.

Hertz, Noreena (2001), *The Silent Take Over*, New York: The Free Press.

Isaak, Robert A. (2005), *The Globalization Gap*, Upper Saddle River, NJ: F T Prentice Hall.

Medawar, P. B. (1959), *The Future of Man*, New York: Mentor Books.

Prahalad, C. K. (2005), *The Fortune At the Bottom of The Pyramid*, Upper Saddle River, NJ: Wharton School Publishing.

Samli, A. Coskun (2002), *In Search of An Equitable, Sustainable Globalization*, Westport, CT: Quorum Books.

Samli, A. Coskun (2004), *Entering and Succeeding In Emerging Countries*, Mason, OH: Thomson, South-Western.

Webster's New Twentieth Century Dictionary, (1968) New York: The Word Publishing Company, 269.

Jacksonville, FL, USA   A.C. Samli

Contents

Introduction

Consider the following two cases: First, in the 18th century, a company with the name Singer emerged. This was one of the very rare companies that made a very strong impact on the well-being of consumers throughout the world. Before the sewing machine, it was very difficult, if not impossible, to sew clothing and other necessities. The important fact is that in the remotest parts of this world still there are many Singer sewing machines that are either empowered by a foot pedal or by a hand crank. From such an invention came local sewing schools, arts and crafts businesses, exporting products of these activities, ready-made apparel production, and many other similar entrepreneurial activities which brought consumer value, created jobs as well as generated modest but reasonable profits. It was an innovation that reached out to the forgotten majority of the world and created much consumer value. This wave of economic force came from top and reached out the forgotten majority of the world. Unchecked top-down incidences such as this one created much economic power at the top which led in the direction of further top-down globalization. But subsequently, this top-down globalization gave way to greed more than just ambition and has been creating much controversial situations that are discussed in this book. It is this global top-down greed factor that has created sweat shops where poor and powerless worked under intolerable conditions, child labor that is exploiting little children in many poorer parts of the world; minimum wages at the subsistence levels became a general happening in the poorest countries, and many other practices that are illegal and inhuman, such as drug trafficking or trafficking women to be used as prostitutes, emerge as unchecked global and extremely lucrative activities.

Second, in the 1970s, a young Turkish student received a scholarship to study textile engineering in Germany. Since his family was engaged in different aspects of textiles, he took a couple of bags full of textiles to sell and earn some spending money. Some 25 years later, with partners in many countries, he has a number of factories creating jobs for local people, and the business is expanding and reaching out to the forgotten majority in many parts of the world. These two cases explain the author's position on bottom-up globalization and international entrepreneurship. In other words, small, local, and ambitious entrepreneurs starting from the bottom and creating consumer value for that population tier are likely to make great contributions toward a better world.

Consider the fact that 5 percent of the American population receives more than 50 percent of the total national income of the country and then expand this concept throughout the world. In most emerging countries, the situation is far worse. Great majorities of the world's population are forgotten. Global giants are trying to generate income and would forget these large groups of people who have not as much money as the rich or the middle class groups in the world. At least Americans don't hate Bill Gates who owns as much as 40 percent of the American population combined. However, the situation is very different in most of the emerging countries. People do not care for the aristocracy which is present everywhere and, much of the time, not very beneficial to the struggles of the large numbers of poor people in those societies. This situation is getting worse as top-down globalization is helping the rich to accumulate more and more economic power. As will be seen throughout this book, the author believes that the most serious problems the earth, which is called the fragile planet in this book, is facing are economics related and that the world's economy, at the point of writing this book, is tied into globalization in an extremely intimate manner. Thus, this book is partially on globalization. But the author takes a different position on globalization than what Friedman (2000) calls Darwinism on steroids. The author believes that a tamer globalization is not only needed but required to make the future of the fragile planet brighter. However, left alone, 21st-century capitalism is likely to do nothing but exacerbate the present situation. It is doubtful that such imbalanced economic activity could be sustainable.

In order to understand my message throughout this book, two opposing points of view regarding markets and functioning within them must be brought to fore. John F. Gaski (1985) stated that

> The "societal marketing" concept, or the view that marketing has a greater social responsibility than just satisfying customers at a profit, is an erroneous and counterproductive idea. For marketers to attempt to serve the best interests of society is not only undemocratic but dangerous as well.

Such statements are widely accepted by 21st-century capitalists who see themselves in the business of making money and nothing else. Their general orientation is that the market is very capable of taking care of itself, and if it is not interfered with, it will function well. Behind this position is the myth that the market is not only natural but almost sacrosanct. This is the justification behind the thinking that, uninterfered with, the market will function perfectly and will yield best results.

The second statement is by William M. Dugger (1989):

> The simple observation that the market is an instituted process rather than a natural equilibrium takes on great significance because it makes accountable men and women who exercise power behind the protection of the market myth. That simple observation eliminates their protection. When the market is understood as an instituted process, those who institute it can be held responsible.

Thus, Dugger points out that the "enabling myths" that empower the upper strata in a society to maintain dominance over the lower are a myth. According to Dugger, those who benefit from the institutionalized status quo believe that they benefit from this situation because their personal gifts or efforts merit it. Furthermore, he maintains that those who are for the status quo in the market and they believe in the fairness of the natural balance of the market do not quite comprehend that: First, people are educable and given the opportunity they can play a critical role in their own destiny, and second, people do not have equal opportunity to economic well-being, intellectual and political advancements. But given a chance for equal opportunity to improve themselves, regardless where they are and who they are, people will do so.

In this book, I posit that unlike the view that the market is a product of divine dispensation that comes very close to the presently prevailing 21st-century capitalism, if the market is improved by what I call *social capitalism*, not only those who are in power will retain their power but the whole world will be better off as well. The future of this fragile planet will become brighter as opposed to the gloom it displays at the present time. If people are educated, economic powers are spread out, and equal opportunity to participate in economic and market activities are made possible, the fragile planet called earth will have a much better chance to survive and improve. Those who have amassed much economic power must use enlightened self-interest and must exercise not *greed* but *ambition*. Thus, the present author puts forth a blueprint for the 21st-century capitalism that is based on Dugger's (1989) position. Throughout this book, the details of such a blueprint are presented. The author maintains that the powerful ongoing globalization process must be altered to facilitate a bright future for the fragile planet.

I believe that a tamer globalization that reaches out to the lower layers of the global economic pyramid of the world, based on slightly modified capitalism, can be achieved by utilizing three key concepts: social capitalism, bottom-up globalization, and entrepreneurship. Social capitalism is a more spread-out version of capitalism that is not based on greed and which encourages ambition and positive aspects of competition. However, the author also believes that the already accumulated excessive economic power in the 21st century is leading in the direction of accumulating more economic power at any cost. This type of orientation, based on the concept of Darwinism on steroids, is creating a shocking and accelerating discrepancy between the economic status of haves and have-nots. It is critical that the benefits of technology reach larger groups of people throughout the world. Better infrastructures must be developed in the emerging countries. Access to education must be equal throughout the world. Environmental responsibility is understood and shared by all nations, all authorities, and all companies. A reasonable, fair, but progressive taxation system must be adopted and practiced so that infrastructures and social services such as health and education can be financed. Investments should take place to improve emerging economies. Companies must develop a better way to share the gains of businesses with all the participants, rather than only a few executives or stockholders. And competition in markets and industries must be encouraged to become more powerful and encourage creativity and innovation rather than throwing brute economic power around. Poorer countries must be encouraged to concentrate more on endogenous development rather than waiting and hoping for help from outside only.

Practicing social capitalism, in addition to practicing ambition rather than greed, will call for what the author coins bottom-up globalization. Here small, ambitious, and entrepreneurial companies will partner across the national boundaries to reach out to the remote corners of world markets. In so doing, they will balance the extreme powers of top-down globalization. It must be posited here also that such a balance will minimize global terrorism possibilities which are occupying the industrialized countries excessively as this book is being written. The author believes that economic fairness that can be brought about by social capitalism is a key weapon against international terrorism.

Finally, the author also believes that entrepreneurship that is based on local utilization of modern technologies and creating wealth, consumer value, and jobs at local levels must take place to support the bottom-up globalization. *Creative constructionism* presented by entrepreneurship must be in place to take care of economic discrepancies between the haves and have-nots. The author maintains that capitalism is at its best when it is benefiting not a select few, but all. Modern globalization is a very critical tool to be used positively at this juncture. AND HERE IS HOW.

References

Dugger, William M. (1989), "Instituted Process and Enabling Myth: The Two Faces of the Market," *Journal of Economic Issues*, June, 607–615.

Friedman, Thomas (2000), *The Lexus and the Olive Tree*, New York: Anchor.

Gaski, John (1985), "Dangerous Territory: The Social Marketing Concept Revisited," *Business Horizons*, July/August, 42–47.

Chapter 1
The Dismal World Picture

At the dawn of the 21st century when we know more about the world and about poverty; when we can communicate with people who live in the remotest parts of the world in a matter of seconds through the Internet; when we know the environmental hazards of certain industrial activity; when we know more than ever before about other cultures, other values than ours, and other lifestyles than ours; and finally, when we can deliver bombs that can destroy the world instantly by our planes that are faster than sound and perhaps lightening, why are we not able to say this world is better off today than ever before?

A Merrill Lynch ad said, "The spread of free markets and democracy around the world is permitting more people everywhere to turn their aspirations into achievements." Certainly these are wonderful words. If only they had some substance. Again, at the dawn of the 21st century when geographic borders and, perhaps, human borders are disappearing, progress is not taking place. Globalization, which is a very powerful weapon in transferring information, technology, funds, and know-how to anywhere in the world, is not delivering what it promised. As it expands and gains power, globalization is causing the disappearance of geographic borders by making global trading easier than ever before and bringing the trading people from different countries and different cultures closer together. Proponents of globalization maintained that as different parties of the world converge economically and politically, the living standards of richer and poorer nations will also converge. However, this wishful thinking did not materialize (Hertz 2001). As Friedman (2000, p. 279) states, "...globalization as a culturally homogenizing and environment-devouring is coming on" extremely fast. It can easily wipe out the ecological and cultural identities of the nations that took thousands if not millions of years of evolutionary progress (Friedman 2000). The disappearance of geographic and human borders unchecked is benefiting only a few privileged people around the globe and causing disaster for vast numbers of human beings. Instead of having a philosophy of "no one should be left behind," the philosophy of "let them eat cake" prevails. Thus, the fragile planet named Earth is becoming a military or economic war zone. In either case, in the long run, everybody loses.

A.C. Samli, *Globalization from the Bottom Up*,
DOI: 10.1007/978-0-387-77098-7_1, © Springer Science+Business Media, LLC 2008

Abject Poverty

It is extremely difficult for an upper middle class person in the North American continent or in Western Europe to imagine, but the fact is that approximately 1.6 billion people in the world are living on less than one dollar a day. It is estimated that another billion people manage their day-to-day living with less than two dollars a day. In some very poor parts of Africa, local languages do not have future tenses since people are simply struggling to survive one day at a time and hence have never thought of the future.

Not only is the world not better off today, but the worsening process is accelerating. As Chua (2003, p. 9) states, "...the global spread of markets and democracy is a principal, aggravating cause of group hatred and ethnic violence throughout the non-Western world." We in the Western world may not realize that our concepts of markets, profits, and democracies may not be acceptable in many parts of the world.

From the bag ladies of Waikiki to the slums of Mexico to garbage picking children in Sri Lanka, millions are barely surviving a lifestyle that cannot be called humane or described as human. The discrepancy between the poor and the rich has become mind-boggling. As Chua (2003) states, in the year 2000, DeBeers, one of the most well-known names in diamond trading, recovered about 570,000 carats of high-quality diamonds off the Namibian coast. They may have over 600 million dollars of street value. At that time, about 60 percent Namibians had no access to sanitary toilets. Resources are owned by big companies and are used for them to improve their own profit pictures and enhance their own economic powers. The proceeds of such activities are not shared with the people at the lower end of that country. The picture, simply, is not much different throughout the world. Just what is causing poverty? The World Bank (2001) identifies eight causes of poverty:

- Lack of income and wealth to obtain basic necessities such as food, shelter, clothing, adequate health care and education.
- Not having a voice or power in state and other social institutions.
- Extreme vulnerability to unexpected and devastating shocks such as earthquakes, tsunamis, etc.
- Not having human assets such as labor skills or health-related issues.
- Not having natural assets such as land.
- Not having physical assets that would connect them to the infrastructure.
- Less than adequate financial assets such as savings or having access to credit.
- Absence of social assets such as networks, support systems, and the like.

World Development Report (2001).

These conditions are all self-explanatory. There has been detailed discussion of some of these items (Isaak 2005), however, the critical issue here is that none of these eight items indicate a specific solution or where the society may go to remedy these desperate situations. Describing hopelessness and helplessness does not lead in the direction of positive action. And a favorite statement of this author is that wishful thinking is not a strategy which should always be kept in mind by those who are making critical decisions for the future of this world. Without some serious positive action, the prevailing conditions are getting worse.

Just What Is Happening to the Haves and Have-Nots

Within countries as well as between countries, the discrepancy between the rich and the poor is becoming so great that it is mind-boggling. At no time in history have so few amassed so much economic power and wealth. Perhaps the most unfortunate part of this dismal story is that although economies are not zero-sum games in that one party's loss is the other party's gain, they are treated as such. Instead of progress so that both parties, i.e., the rich and the poor, make progress and enjoy economic gains, the rich are getting richer and the poor are becoming poorer. Much of this is due to the fact that global capitalism and "market democracies" totally favor the rich and the rich are not necessarily inclined to share their riches with the poor. Indeed, in recent years, owing to increased productivity along with cost cutting through international outsourcing of jobs, the corporate profitability of global giants has consistently been in the double digits. In the meantime, these giants are inclined to lay off workers, not to raise wages, while they have been giving obscene increases and benefit packages to their top managements.

In the meantime, as foreign companies or their local partners enter into the picture, they are making the traditional labor-intensive industries obsolete and popularizing capital-intensive and more efficient industries. This process is eliminating the traditional labor-intensive jobs that have been given to those unskilled and uneducated majorities in third world countries. Thus, while some are becoming much more than gainfully employed, many, many others are becoming totally unemployed. Again, here lies the bipolarization of the world's population. Isaak (2005) calls this "the globalization gap." Perhaps the worst thing about this gap is that it is not constant and is getting worse.

If we put all of these trends into a comprehensive picture, the have-nots today are, more than ever before in the world, becoming *have-nothings*. Contrariwise, haves today, relatively speaking, are smaller in numbers but are incomparably wealthier and are, therefore, becoming *have-mores*. As such, they are gaining more power and influencing world and domestic politics and causing serious hostilities that are threatening the future of the fragile planet even further (Samli 2002).

Exhibit 1.1 illustrates the dismal situation. While per capita income in Switzerland is almost $41,000, it is only $200 in Mozambique. This discrepancy is rather difficult to comprehend in the 21st century. This situation is, if anything, getting worse.

As stated earlier, about 1.6 billion people in the world today who are living on about one dollar day, and another one billion people who are estimated to be living on about 2 dollars a day, are extremely unhappy. Their hopelessness cannot help but exacerbate the ill feelings they develop toward the rich and powerful. It is difficult to imagine a peaceful world with such discrepancies between the rich and the poor.

Exhibit 1.1 Per capita income (in dollars) of five richest and five poorest countries (1998)

Rich countries		Poor countries	
Switzerland	40,820	Mozambique	200
Norway	34,710	Chad	230
Japan	33,720	Nigeria	290
Denmark	32,770	Sudan	300
United States	30,700	Zambia	330

Source: www.worldbank.org

It is maintained by many social thinkers that widening economic gap between the haves and have-nots will instigate more international terrorism and domestic class warfare.

Middle Class Is Withering Away

It has been argued that the middle class in societies maintains stability and continuity. However, first, most third world countries barely have a middle class and, second, in most Western economies the middle class is shrinking. The end result of the lack or disappearance of the middle class is that this most stabilizing factor in societies is or is becoming absent. As the gap between the rich and the poor widens, the lack of a middle class as a buffer between the two becomes more serious. Without such a stabilizing factor, it is easier for some variation of class warfare to commence. History is full of such examples and clearly the lessons from history have not been learned. As can be seen, emergence and maintenance of a middle class is not just a nice and desirable development. It is a *must* if societies and, indeed, the world desire to have stability. Without political, social, and economic stability, it is not possible for a society to make progress. Indeed, the world is composed of multiple societies and, if they do not make progress, the world stands still. Consistently, the two extremes, haves and have-nots, will clash, first in deeds, actions, and dealings, but eventually this clash may become a civil war or some kind of revolution, the impact of which would be rather devastating. Skocpol (2000) articulates the American scene as follows:

> American social policy once addressed the needs and values of most citizens (is now) battered by an aging population, growing income inequality, and the troubling impact on our children of overworked, underpaid, or single parents, social supports have become increasingly fragmented and widely perceived as ineffective. (from the front jacket)

If the situation in the most powerful and wealthy society in the world is as gloomy-sounding as this, one may question what is happening in the rest of the world. Or stated more dramatically: What is the future of this fragile planet?

The importance of a present and thriving middle class or an emerging one is taken very seriously in this book. A thriving middle class is not only a stabilizing factor within the society, but it is also an indicator of economic growth and fairness of the distribution of economic wealth. If there is a middle class, it may mean that those who are very poor still have a remote possibility of moving up to the middle class ranks.

Lester C. Thurow (1996) discusses the possibility of American capitalism imploding because its social organization is not generating the wealth that is somewhat more fairly distributed and, therefore, even the American middle class is dissipating. This implies the need for a stronger and thriving middle class in the industrial world and the need for the emergence of a middle class in the third world. But if the middle class is dissipating in the strongest market economy in the world, it will be futile to assume that the same middle class will take its rightful place in the world and maintain that place. It is simply not very logical to expect thriving middle classes to emerge automatically throughout the world under the prevailing conditions of the 21st-century capitalism.

The Need for a Middle Class

The need for a middle class has always been articulated as an important phenomenon in sociological and economic analyses of societies. However, the urgency of generating and empowering the middle class takes a different orientation in this book. This urgency primarily stems from two different but strongly related analyses. First, Kotler, Jatusripitak, and Maesincee (1997) have put forth a theory of actively participating intelligentsia. And the second theory is market-dominant minorities presented by Chua (2003). That intelligentsia in South Korea, for example, borrowed the technology from Japan and, in return, produced for Japan for a number of years, and as a result of these exchanges, companies like Samsung and Emerson emerged. Without such technology transfer, it is questionable if South Korea could have achieved its current economic status.

Actively participating intelligentsia is maintained to be the prime mover of economic development. The experiences of Singapore, Hong Kong, and Taiwan are all along the lines of South Korea. These four countries have been referred to as the "four tigers of Asia." These countries have all done very well in terms of reversing abject poverty to respectable riches. Capable, ambitious, and well-off intelligentsias have maintained a hands-on economic activity which created a thriving middle class.

The market-dominant minorities refer to the presence of certain small groups in the society that have performed extremely well in the respective markets of certain countries. Jews in Russia, the Chinese in Indonesia, and European whites in South Africa are typical examples. These dominant minorities also have been maintaining a hands-on economic involvement and helping the emergence of a middle class. In both cases, i.e., actively participating intelligentsia and market-dominant minorities, the elite as well as other market-dominant minorities are extremely entrepreneurial, well-educated, proactive, and successful. Their presence stimulates the emergence of the balancing middle class. If there is no middle class to function as a buffer to balance the economy and facilitate growth, the two groups invariably clash. The presence of the middle class eases the animosity between the two extremes and, again, indicates to the poor that they do have a chance to become part of the middle class. Motivating the poor to work harder in this fashion is a critical step in the direction of economic development.

Insecurity and Clash of Civilizations

Globalization has been proceeding at full speed. As globalization reaches, selectively, many poor countries, if these countries do not have a fully active accomplished intelligentsia or a reasonably friendly market-dominant minority, it wreaks havoc. As Thomas Friedman (2000) put it, globalization is Darwinism on steroids. This is a statement we refer to throughout this book, directly or indirectly a number of times. As such, globalization without these two groups, intelligentsia and minorities, and a supporting buffer group of an existing or emerging middle class, would create a very uncomfortable situation for the have-nots.

As capital-intensive technologies through globalization sweep away the traditionally labor-intensive industries and create a few good jobs and eliminate many, many labor-intensive jobs, insecurity in these societies sets in. Without an elite or buffer group of middle class providing some stability for society, globalization creates much insecurity, hatred, and hostility because, first and foremost, it is taking away the traditional labor-intensive jobs and giving almost nothing in return.

Second, technology and globalization also challenge traditional values, local cultures, and the authority of local governments. As unchecked and unadministered global capitalism spreads, national and local governments are being stripped of their powers and reduced to the status of mere spectators (Hertz 2001). As a result, globalization creates a clash of civilizations which intensifies local hostilities against "foreigners" who are bringing these technologies and eliminating jobs. Thus, the head-on collision of traditional and modern values becomes not only explosive, but also reinforces extremism. People in all cultures unite as they see a common enemy. Here the dismal picture gets worse as traditionalists not only unite, but also start thinking of and planning revenge. When outside values, that are not familiar or acceptable, along with the entry or presence of powerful foreigners, start invading the prevailing culture in remote parts of the third world, and when this is construed to be a major threat to the existence of the masses, extremists manage to unite people against a common enemy.

As hostilities become real and lines of demarcation are clearly drawn, people unite against a common enemy. This unification often takes place in the form of religious zealotry. The history of mankind indicates many, many conflicts and wars that are partially or fully religion based. Unfortunately, in such cases it really is not the religion itself but religious extremists who call the shots to gain power and to control people. They have much to gain physically, economically and, in fact, in their warped minds, spiritually, by pitting societies and cultures against each other. At the point of writing this book, religious animosity in the world is almost at its peak. It appearsthat Christianity is declaring war on the Muslim extremists under the guise of terrorism and vice versa. If not checked and controlled, the current dismal picture that has been discussed thus far will be almost nothing in comparison to what could happen if a major religion-inspired war were to take place. If intervention does not occur, this clash of civilizations, even though it is in its early stages at this point in time, is likely to become extremely explosive in the forthcoming decades. Although it is expected that the "magical combination of free markets and democracy would transform the world into a community of modernized, peace-loving nations, and individuals into civic-minded citizens and consumers," this is totally blocked by "ethnic hatred, religious zealotry and other backward aspects of underdevelopment" (Chua 2003, from the front jacket). The clash of cultures is not only a barrier to progress but also the igniter of global terrorism yet to emerge.

The Prospect of Class Warfare

While the clash of cultures is in the making internationally, domestically many emerging countries are not at peace within themselves. Globalization, via foreign direct investments (FDI) and information technology, creates a new group of very rich, powerful, and shrewd industrialists, and leaves the majority behind. Again, without having the buffer of the middle class and the proactive elite, the hands-on function of which is benevolent, the picture is bound to become dimmer. Civil unrest in Haiti, in Sudan, the current situations in Iraq, Iran, and Chechnya and many other countries could partly or fully develop into class warfare within these countries. A few people succeeding spectacularly through globalization within the country will not be looked upon favorably by those who are not benefiting and, if there is no dedicated elite or middle class buffer to ease the situation, the situation is likely to become extremely explosive.

Treating the Symptoms Rather than the Causes

As this book is being written, perhaps the most important international issue is terrorism. Most industrialized countries are developing counter-terrorism plans and strategies. Part of the terrorism activity is definitely incited by what the author is discussing here. Insecurity combined with the economic discrepancies among the classes in civilizations, by definition, provides a fertile ground for terrorism. Just what is being done to stop this activity can easily be questioned. Generating more military power, passing laws that limit individual freedoms, and putting billions of dollars into intelligence are hardly solutions. They are unfortunate ploys to win elections. These measures make all parties very unhappy, since they limit freedoms and do not enhance global understanding. These reactionary solutions are primarily based on simplistic explanations of the prevailing hostilities such as "they hate us for what we are." If they hate us, it may be because of what we might have done to them even though it may not have been intentional. Here "us" can be applicable to any explosive situation, meaning that a simplistic explanation of international hostilities does not help explain the causes and, hence, deters a deeper understanding of the problem which might lead to a reasonable solution. Experience indicates that we cannot establish peace and understanding by brute power alone.

If there are clear-cut causes of international terrorism, it cannot be stopped by *reactive solutions* such as the ones mentioned above. Instead of reactive solutions, there must be *proactive measures* that will eliminate international terrorism. Here

the most important consideration is to get to the root causes of terrorism and eliminate them. In a situation where the poor get much poorer and the rich get much
richer, resentment and hostility get kindled. Particularly if natives know (or at least
think) that the recessions and the booms in their economy are fueled by foreigners, it
does not take much to develop frustration, hatred, and anger. Sachs (2004) maintains
that if America were to spend small amounts toward promoting Africa's economy,
she would save billions of dollars from counter-terrorism activities and would make
the West more secure. He restates the old saying, "One ounce of prevention will be
worth a ton of treatment."

Here, arms, military intelligence, or other similar measures do nothing to prevent
such hostility. The solutions lie in bridging the gap between the rich and the poor,
both domestically and internationally. Informing and educating the masses to avoid
helplessness and to look for opportunities, and developing opportunities for those
who have had nothing up to now, would be very helpful along with proactive
measures. At the writing of this book, none of these remedies are considered seriously. Instead, more and more resources are put into the military which, in itself,
is intimidating and hostility-creating. People do not like power unless it is theirs.
In this case, it is not theirs. Certainly, such narrow vision contributes more to the
dismal picture that this small and fragile planet called Earth is emanating at this
point in time, and there is no relief in sight.

Proactivity Matters

Throughout this book, the author analyzes the dismal picture that is being projected
by this fragile planet. As the dismal problems are articulated, in every specific issue,
arguments are also presented as to how we (a general "we" representing world
leaders and their thinking) do not understand the seriousness of the issues and how
we take a posture of inactive or reactive rather than proactive. When President Bush
articulated preemptive strategies against terrorism, he was still being reactive. Truly
preemptive strategies against terrorism will be the development and implementation
of proactive strategies that will attack and eliminate the root causes of global discontent and hostilities. This will take a major change in the thinking and orientation of
a vast group of leaders who explicitly or implicitly dwell upon questionable orientations such as: "My God can beat your God," "My army can beat yours any time," "I
am clearly better than you," "Be reasonable, do it my way, or else." The arrogance
goes as far as one nation calling some other nations "rogue" nations. This shows not
only arbitrariness but also snobbery which is uncalled for. Throughout this book,
I explore alternative orientations and proactive solutions. Our positions are based
on trying to establish an order on unchecked and undirected political and market
activities which simply do not generate the proper conditions that would rectify the
prevailing dismal picture. In fact, a "laissez-faire" type of overall world activity will
certainly favor those who have much wealth and power already. But these people
who are extremely powerful are not inclined to actively act on "no person should
be left behind." They are not necessarily involved in developing the economy in

such a way that it would help all and not only a few privileged parties or groups. Therefore, a reasonable guidance is needed to ease capitalistic imperialism and to create a *benevolent capitalism* or, as discussed in this book, a *social capitalism*.

Micromanaging Macroissues Does Not Pay

As the 20th-century capitalism under the pressures of the greed factor moved in the direction of gaining more power, privatization was advocated. This push for privatization led in the direction of micromanaging macroissues. Some of the dramatic consequences of such practices are:

- Progress is hindered by too much emphasis on private education for profit and not enough access to education on the part of the people with limited means.
- Environmental activities are looked at as a cost factor by many private sector activists as opposed to a major economic stimulant by the government.
- Progressiveness of income tax is reduced which made it impossible to deal with deteriorating infrastructures, basic research, and education for all.
- Global giants, instead of expanding investing and developing economies, prefer mergers and acquisitions which cause reduction in competition and very deep downsizing in major employment areas.
- Giving unnecessary tax cuts along with giving 500 percent increases to management salaries created tremendous hardship and disincentives in the workforce.
- The private sector, in its micromanagement mode, is not providing great opportunities for the much-needed entrepreneurial activity.

It must be understood that all societies have macro and microissues. Both are important. But when macro (or societal) issues are handled in a manner of micromanagement by private groups, greed as usual enters into the picture as opposed to the needed solutions to macroissues to benefit the whole society. Unfortunately, greed is oriented toward benefiting just certain select groups.

The Greed Factor

Ideally, capitalism "allows individuals to choose how they allocate their time, where (and if) they work, and what they do with their money they earn" (Hicks 2004). In the 19th century when capitalism was coming into its own, this particular orientation was quite constructive. It stimulated ambition, and many ambitious competitors struggled to better themselves and, concomitantly, they made a contribution to the society's betterment as well. At least partly, because of the competition factor, parties had to work hard and had to excel to improve their economic position. This did not work nearly as well as it was hoped for all, but it worked well enough. And ambition as an outcome as well as a stimulating factor in economic well-being made a significant contribution in Western Europe and, particularly, in North America.

In the 21st-century capitalism, however, there are very powerful economic forces, along with extremely lucrative opportunities, that create a special zeal to pursue material gains not necessarily by ambition and resultant hard work through economic activity, but by greed and the resultant perception of seeing the world as a zero-sum game. Pursuing material gains in the 21st-century capitalism revolves more around gaining at the expense of other human goals and activities (Hicks 2004). Thus, whereas Ayn Rand stated "greed is actually good" (Hanson 2004), it is questionable that she made a distinction between greed and ambition. In the 21st-century capitalism, greed is causing many problems with global giants behaving in their questionable manner. Many global giants are neither acting accountable to shareholders nor to stakeholders or to the masses of bystanders. In the dawn of the 21st century, there have been more CEO scandals and ruthless treatment of workers in these corporate entities than ever before. Enron and Worldcom fiascos are typical examples of how 21st-century capitalism can go out of control and injure masses. The global giants especially like their global activities which are very profitable since they have little, if any, competition, very few rules to be followed, and almost no enforcement of any authority. In the name of capitalism in the 21st century, the greed factor is winning over the ambition factor.

If the greed factor is the engine of expected social progress but is not based on some degree of enlightened self-interest, then the assumption of the presence of a zero-sum society becomes the crux of the matter (Wachtel 2003). This means that blind selfishness will emasculate the possibilities of a fair and widespread economic growth. Whereas the ambition factor is reasonably constructive and rewarding both to the individual and the society, the greed factor, although possibly very lucrative to the individual, can be and in most cases is extremely destructive to the society. It is even more so globally, since stakes are greater and controls are even weaker. It is maintained in this book that most of the problems of the fragile society are stemming from the unchecked greed factor. If we were to pursue the grand ambition of building a better world, it will be necessary to check the greed factor and replace it with the ambition factor. Although in recent years much has been said and done in the area of ethics, primarily in academic circles, the author believes that the most effective way of controlling the greed factor is competition. Competitive forces stop individuals' taking advantage of others. Competition stimulates creativity and the will to survive and excel. The 21st-century capitalism, because of its overwhelming obsession with merger mania, has been systematically reducing competitiveness in domestic and world markets (Samli 2002). Additionally, in the 19th-century capitalism, there were important laws, such as antitrust laws, that made sure that competition continued and even strengthened. However, starting with the last two decades of the 20th century and continuing in the 21st century, deregulation has become the popular practice. Deregulation has created lawlessness. In the absence of laws and regulations, the ambition factor gives way to the greed factor. Those who have the power will enhance their economic base at any cost to the society. Whereas some of the laws are eliminated under the rubric of deregulation, those that are still in the books are not enforced. The greed factor thus finds a way of expanding throughout the world. This situation gives a bad name to capitalism that otherwise would be a powerful tool for economic success.

A Comparative Analysis

Exhibit 1.2 contrasts greed and ambition. In this contrast, six dimensions are utilized: constructive atmosphere, perception of the world, personality traits, time dimension, civic-mindedness, and selfishness.

A brief discussion of these six dimensions are presented here. It must be reiterated that there is only a thin line between greed and ambition. All ambitious people, as their gains become significant, can become greedy. However, the thin line that exists between the two can be considered as the *destroyer* or the*savior* of the fragile planet.

Constructive Atmosphere

The greed factor displays itself in the form of a "get them before they get you" mentality. It drives individuals to win in any way, shape, or form. It brings about the

Exhibit 1.2 A contrast between greed and ambition

Greed factor	Ambition factor
Constructive atmosphere	
Get them before they get you. Win anyway you can but that will be stepping on many bodies	Working and collaborating with people. There is room for improvement and opportunity for everyone
Perception of the world	
Get as much as you can get at any cost. It is already there. You cannot change the world, exploit it	There could be much progress and that could be very beneficial individually. You can change the world and benefit from it
Personality traits	
Mean, grabbing, I got mine you do whatever you do as long as you don't stand in my way orientation	Generous, sharing knowledge and opportunity. Working with others and allowing others to raise themselves as they raise him/her
Time dimension	
What do we want? Everything. When do we want it? Now. There is no time	There is time for improvement and advancement. We can wait as long as we are making progress. There is enough time
Civic-mindedness	
I don't care about the environment, I don't care about pollution, I don't care about the poor. I must make as much as possible	If the environment is improved, if poor have more money, I will be better off also
Selfishness element	
Must get all that I can for the number one (me). This should not have any limits. My doing better is my activity and will be done	There is enough talent for progress. If the society is improving I will do even better. My doing better depends on many others doing better as well

feeling that the greedy person's advancement depends on how many people he/she can walk over.

The ambition factor, on the other hand, generates the feeling that working and collaborating with other people enhances opportunities for progress. Here the understanding is that there is room for advancement not only for one person at the expense of many others, but there is room for progress and opportunity for all.

Perception of the World

The greed factor moves in the direction of getting everything one can get. The world is developed, and getting anything basically means taking things away from others. Since the world is developed, our advancement will be based on others' loss.

The ambition factor, however, advocates that there is much progress to be made and that progress can be very good for all participants. While the world can be changed and improved, all people can benefit from such change and improvement.

Personality Traits

The personality characteristics of those under the spell of the greed factor are such that they are selfish and somewhat mean. They think in terms of "I must get mine whatever it takes, and nobody should stand in my way." Again, people who are motivated by the ambition factor have different personality traits. They are generous, sharing knowledge and information about existing and potential opportunities. They work with others and let others also advance as they advance themselves.

Time Dimension

People motivated by the greed factor want everything and want it now. There is no time to waste and, therefore, it should not be wasted.

Ambitious people, on the other hand, realize that there is time for improvement. In fact, good performance and advancement take time. We can wait, they would think, as long as there is progress. There is enough time for everything.

Civic-Mindedness

The greed factor group does not pay any attention to the environment. They see environmental efforts as costly and unnecessary. The orientation typically is "I don't care about pollution, nor do I care about the poor and downtrodden. I must make as much money as possible."

The ambitious group takes the position that if the environment is improved and pollution is reduced, this will mean more jobs, more money, and other benefits for all. And if the poor have more money, they will buy more of my goods and services which will be good for all concerned.

Selfishness Element

Here the orientation of the greedy is "must get all what I can for the number one (me)." This should not have any limits and any barriers. I must do better. That is my goal and it will be done. Whatever happens to other people is their problem.

The ambitious element, however, considers the fact that there is much talent out there and that the whole society will benefit from the utilization of this talent. Progress is team work, and working with others is synergistic.

Exhibit 1.2 illustrates two extreme pictures of greed and ambition. However, it must also be reiterated that at one point there is only a fine line between the two. It is reasonable to presume that all human beings can be ambitious, and this ambition could develop in an extreme level to greed. At this point it can be posited that unchecked ambition, once it reaches a certain level of success, could easily turn into greed. As once was stated brilliantly, power corrupts, and absolute power corrupts absolutely. When Bill Gates developed the preliminaries of Windows in a dorm room, it was ambition. However, as some courts, both in the United States as well as in Europe claim, this ambition turned into greed as Microsoft started using its power in an abusive manner and exercising a stifling monopoly over competition and competitors. In the following two chapters, a number of cases are proposed as the results of the greed factor, and the meaning of these cases is discussed as to their impact on the fragile planet called *Earth*.

Differences in the Practices

Exhibit 1.3 illustrates the critical contradictions between the practices of the greedy and the practices of the ambitious. It is clear that whereas the ambition factor can be very constructive for the future of the fragile planet, the greed factor can be devastating.

The greedy try to minimize or eliminate competition by mergers or acquisitions; the ambitious increase competition and employment by expansion. From this perspective, it is possible to posit that greed is the enemy of ambition. Ambitious and successful newly emerging small businesses are being gobbled up by greedy corporate pirates.

The greedy limit the pay of subordinates, thinking that there will be more remaining for them. The ambitious, on the other hand, hope to generate a better distribution of income so that the markets will also be greater.

The greedy will outsource only to lower costs so that there will be more remaining for them. The ambitious will outsource to improve quality and the participation of others so that consumer surplus can be maximized.

Exhibit 1.3 Differences in the practices of the greedy versus ambitious

Practices of the greedy	Practices of the ambitious
Likes to expand by buying out competition or through mergers (reduces competition and employment)	Likes to expand by starting new plants or by new production activity (increases competition and employment)
Blocks increases in minimum wages. Gives unrealistic raises only to those who are very rich and powerful	Encourages better distribution of income and progress of workers and lower management
Outsources not to improve quality or the participation of others but to maximize the share of the profits that goes to the top management	Outsources to improve quality and the participation of others. Builds advantage in collaborating with others
Uses its power to receive greater favors from the political bodies	Emphasizes spreading the power base to reach out to as many as possible so that the poor and underprivileged will do better as the profit base increases
Does not share proceeds with those who contribute much to the profitability in a proportionate manner. Believes in keeping as much of the proceeds as possible	Shares proceeds with all the others proportionate to their contribution knowing well that there will be even greater gains in the near future

The greedy will use their economic powers to receive unfair and excessive favors from the existing political establishments. The ambitious will be engaged in spreading the power base as much as possible so that equal opportunity for the poor and underprivileged will be expanded.

The greedy will not share the profits with those who helped them. The ambitious will consider the contribution of all of the involved proportionately so that there will be greater profits in the future that are shared more equitably.

Summary

In its current ways, globalization and capitalism are not reaching out and benefiting the world population. The discrepancy between haves and have-nots clearly is getting worse. This chapter in discussing capitalism makes and attempt to distinguish between "ambition" and "greed." Both of these features are imbedded in capitalism. However, the chapter posits that whereas in the 19th century, capitalism gave rise to ambition and made satisfactory economic progress possible, in the 21st century, capitalism has become the playfield of greed. As a result, conditions in terms of the gap between the rich and the poor, is becoming worse.

References

Chua, Amy (2003), *World On Fire*, New York: Doubleday.
Friedman, Thomas L. (2000), *The Lexus and The Olive Tree*, New York: Achor Books.
Hanson, M. B. (2004), "Ayn Rand Inspired High-Tech Capitalism," *Insight on the News*, September 22, 16–18, The Christian Century, March 23, 24–28.

Hertz, Noreena (2001), *The Silent Take Over*, New York: The Free Press.

Hicks, Douglas A. (2004), *Taming the Best: Virtues of Corporate Life*.

Isaak, Robert A. (2005), *The Globalization Gap*, Upper Saddle River, N.J.: Prentice Hall.

Kotler, Philip, Jatusripitak, Somkid, and Maesincee, Suvit (1997), *The Marketing of Nations*, New York: The Free Press.

Sachs, Jeffrey (2004), "Doing the Sums on Africa," *The Economist*, May 22, 19–21.

Samli, A. Coskun (2002), *In Search of Sustainable, Equitable Globalization*, Westport, CT: Quorum Books.

Skocpol, Theda (2000), *The Missing Middle*, New York: W. W. Norton & Company.

Thurow, Lester C. (1996), *The Future of Capitalism*, New York: Harper Collins Publishers.

Wachtel, Paul L. (2003), "Full Pockets, Empty Lives: A Psychoanalytic Exploration of the Contemporary Culture of Greed," *The American Journal of Psychoanalysis*, June 2003, 103–233.

Chapter 2
The Growth of Militarism and Its Cost

As the gap widens between haves and have-nots widens, which is primarily the outcome of the greed factor, globalization further accelerates this situation. A borderless world and freely flowing communications should be the ideals of every optimist. However, unchecked and undirected, freely flowing communications and trade are making a few extremely rich and powerful. This situation, as partially discussed in Chapter 1, is forcing those who are feeling insecure and frustrated to get together and present a common, but hostile, front to the outside world which they think is taking advantage of them. Such hostile divisions have been the foundations of many wars. Between the 1930s and 1990s, approximately 125 wars and conflicts occurred mostly in the third world with about 40 million casualties. During the last decade of the 20th century, there were even more accelerated military activities.

The 20th Century Was the Bloodiest of All

When Brakow (2000) discusses "the greatest generation," unfortunately he is referring to those who have been engaged in wars, as if it had never happened before . He is discussing a world of conflict which is truly troubling. It has been estimated that military expenditures in the third world have quintupled in constant dollars in about 30 years. In many of these countries, military expenditures exceed or are equal to health and education combined (International Monetary Fund 1991). These figures are even more dramatic if the cold war era is considered and the United States and USSR military expenditures are taken into account. Although Eisenhower warned very strongly about the military–industrial complex, America has had an industrial policy of "military and defense industries" for over 50 years (Clark 1994). As the most powerful nation in the world, the military expenditures of the United States are mind-boggling. The United States is number one in the world, with a military budget of almost $400 billion. The American military budget is almost bigger than many of the economies of emerging countries combined. This is not only intimidating to all of these emerging countries but also suspicion-raising as to the intentions of the United States. One does not expect one's friends to be arming to the teeth and still claiming that their intentions are peaceful and friendly. But the gravest danger is if and when this military might becomes terribly opinionated and sees most other

A.C. Samli, *Globalization from the Bottom Up*,
DOI: 10.1007/978-0-387-77098-7_2, © Springer Science+Business Media, LLC 2008

countries or cultures around the world as its nemesis. Such belligerence forces many smaller and insecure third world countries to isolate themselves and try to defend themselves against a future attack. In fact, when President George W. Bush talked about the axis of evil, Iran and North Korea accelerated their activities in developing their nuclear capabilities.

Military Expenditures

Due to increasingly disappearing geographic and people boundaries, certain groups, particularly the poor, are feeling less secure and unprotected. When they perceive that there is an all-out assault on their roots, their culture and their economic well-being, they put themselves totally far away from the lines of demarcation. Their answer is twofold – military and religious zealotry. In both cases, the world is becoming more divided with the increasing animosity at the lines of demarcation which are becoming more and more identifiable. In the 20th century, not only has this world seen the bloodiest of wars in history but also the most prolonged and debilitating cold war. In both hot and cold wars, once again Eisenhower's brilliant statement, "beware the military industrial complex," came into play. The military expenditures of USSR led that country into economic ruination which led to the dissolution of one of the largest empires (if not the largest) in the history of mankind. On the other hand, in the United States, the cold war created a handful of multi-millionaires as the economy favored production and accumulation of sophisticated arms and armament. However, in the meantime, the mighty American economy has also seen an increase in the number of unemployed, an increase in the number of people without health insurance, an increase in the number of businesses failing, and stagnation in the earnings of the middle class. Wars, both cold and hot, have been costly and have created some serious changes in distribution of income in favor of some of the rich industrialists who are involved in the production and industrial-ization of arms. For instance, the earnings of Lockheed Martin (one of the major suppliers of military hardware) amounted to $1.1 billion for 2003, which is more than twice as much as the company's earnings in 2002 (Wall 2004). There could easily be a question as to whether this company is driven by greed or by ambition. Regardless of the answer to this issue, the company is doing extremely well in a warlike atmosphere and certainly would support hawkish behaviors around the world.

This last point needs further explanation. During the preparation era for World War II, military preparedness created almost full employment. In fact, this led some people to say that the only time we can have full employment in the United States is when there is a major war. However, the conditions of that era are not at all compa-rable with the conditions of the defense industries of current times. In early and mid-1940s, defense equipments were very simplistic. Auto factories produced tanks or small planes. Other military supplies were produced with substantially labor-intensive industries that used all the available workers. However, today's military equipment is so sophisticated that only extremely high-tech intensive industries are able to participate in its production. Thus, instead of generating much employment, military equipment and supplies production is creating only a few extremely well-paying jobs.

The Aftermath of the Cold War

When the dust settled down in 1991, there was no USSR and there was only one unchallenged superpower, the United States. Even though, because of the cold war, the United States utilized much of its resources not to improve the quality of life of its citizenry but empower its military might further, the United States came out victorious from the cold war.

Because of the demise of the USSR and subsequent absence of countervailing power, which balanced the military might of the United States for over half a century, the unchallenged dominance of the United States made many countries very nervous. During the cold war era, the presence of the USSR had given some comfort to a number of countries that the United States could not simply do whatever it pleased. But this countervailing power is now almost totally gone. This nervous-ness, combined with the insecurity and clash of civilizations, has led a number of countries to increase their military expenditures to a point of no return. Much domestic restlessness in numerous third world countries also stemmed from the fact that extreme economic hardships were more than partially attributable to mili-tary expenditures. As these countries tried to advance their own military power, they neglected their citizenry's economic well-being. The countries, by using their scarce resources for military purposes, had less than adequate remaining resources for economic advancement.

Until very recently, the United States used its military might sparingly, and American society believed that there would never be a first strike by the United States. The events of September 11 have changed this position. George W. Bush showed his inclination for a preemptive strike in numerous speeches. And, according to many, to display that he means what he says, he attacked Iraq. In the meantime, as mentioned earlier, the concepts of *rogue countries* and *axes of evil* that have been articulated by George W. Bush have made many countries extremely nervous. Problems with Iran and particularly with North Korea reached critical proportions because of the articulation of these concepts. With the lack of communication between the parties and increasing economic disparities, lines of demarcation are becoming more pronounced.

The West is saying suicide bombers are terrorists, and the East is saying the attack of American-made tanks and missiles on civilians is terrorism. At the point of writing this book, communications between the two groups are totally garbled up and this lack of communications has been contributing to insecurity, distrust, and hostile feelings. If the dismal picture described in the first chapter is not going to be stopped from being further expanded out of proportion, then perhaps nothing can make the picture any worse. It appears that very little is being done to open up communications and create a reasonable atmosphere before the clash of civilization becomes a fact. In such a case, no one wins, and there is a reasonable doubt that this fragile planet can survive another all-out war. In fact, the lack of communication and the lack of reasonable discourse have been forcing parties to arm further because without communication, insecurity begets more insecurity. Thus, militarism is growing everywhere and threatening our future wherever we may be. However, as Albert Einstein (1993) once said, "...a permanent peace cannot be prepared by threats but only by the honest attempt to create mutual trust" (p. 15). Unfortunately, such ideas are hardly paid attention to. Perhaps being peaceable is not quite "macho" and is therefore not favored by majorities.

Guns or Butter

The guns or butter argument has been with us for a very long time. It has always been said that countries must decide on one or the other because we cannot have both. However, it has not been discussed openly in recent years. With the expansion of militarism, this concept needs to come to the forefront. As militarism grows in the industrialized Western world, this part of the world does not get much richer, but these countries are not poor, so they can afford large outlays on military if they desire even though the general populations are forced to sacrifice in terms of their economic betterment. On the other hand, feeling insecure and hostile, the third world countries that need economic progress and improved quality of life are foregoing these very critical options by putting much more emphasis on the military than they can afford. A meaningless arms race with the winners and losers already established but without a finish line has been going on. The fact that such a race may lead to undesirable situations is not adequately discussed. Thus, militarism is gaining power exponentially.

It has been estimated a number of times that what the United States and USSR put into military preparedness during the cold war could have eliminated poverty from the face of this world. But, instead of stopping, it appears that the cold war in a different form with different objectives is not only continuing but also expanding at an accelerated rate. Some global corporate giants are profiting from this accelerating activity. If these global giants are left alone, there may never be a solution to accelerating militarism and hostilities until the world may be destroyed by an all-out war.

Exhibit 2.1 illustrates how big some of the military budgets are. These budgets represent guns and not butter. The U.S. budget is not only the largest in the world, but it is also the largest in peace time in this country. However, since it is only less than four percent of the total GDP of the country, it may not be considered totally outrageous. When the U.S. budget is compared with that of Russia, having the second largest military outlay, it becomes clear that the remnants of the cold war are still present. A military budget of over 19 percent of the total GDP implies a tremendous outlay and economic burden that will set the Russian economy back further. Japan also appears to be putting much of its resources into military activity. Knowing that during much of the era after World War II, the Japanese were not

Exhibit 2.1 Largest military budgets

Selected countries	Military budget (billion)	GDP	% GDP
United States	$396.1	$10.1 trillion	3.92
Russia*	$60.0	$310 billion	19.35
China*	$42.0	$1.2 trillion	3.5
Japan	$40.4	$4.1 trillion	10.15
United Kingdom	$34.0	$1.4 trillion	2.43
Saudi Arabia	$27.2	$186.5 billion	14.58
France	$25.3	$1.3 trillion	1.95
Germany	$21.0	$1.8 trillion	1.17
Brazil*	$17.9	$509 billion	3.52
India	$15.6	$482 billion	3.24
Italy	$15.5	$1.1 trillion	1.41
South Korea	$11.8	$427 billion	2.76
Iran	$9.1	$114 billion	7.98
Israel	$9.0	$100 billion	9.0
Taiwan	$8.2	$280 billion	2.93
Canada	$7.7	$695 billion	1.11
Spain	$6.9	$582 billion	1.19
Australia	$6.6	$369 billion	1.79
Netherlands	$5.6	$380 billion	1.47
Turkey	$5.1	$145 billion	3.52
Singapore	$4.3	$85 billion	5.06
Sweden	$4.2	$210 billion	2.0
United Arab Emirates*	$3.9	$47 billion	8.3
Poland	$3.7	$183 billion	2.02
Greece	$3.3	$117 billion	2.82
Argentina*	$3.1	$269 billion	1.15
Pakistan	$2.6	$59 billion	4.41
Norway	$2.8	$166 billion	1.69
Kuwait	$2.6	$33 billion	7.88
Denmark	$2.4	$162 billion	1.48
Belgium	$2.2	$230 billion	0.96
Colombia	$2.1	$82 billion	2.56
Egypt	$2.1	$99 billion	2.12
Vietnam	$1.8	$33 billion	5.45
Iraq	$1.4	$28 billion	5.0
North Korea	$1.3	$22 billion	5.91
Portugal	$1.3	$110 billion	1.18
Libya	$1.2	$32 billion	3.75
Czech Republic	$1.1	$57 billion	1.93
Philippines	$1.1	$71 billion	1.55
Luxembourg	$0.9	$18.5 billion	4.86
Hungary	$0.8	$52 billion	1.54
Syria	$0.8	$20 billion	4.0
Cuba	$0.7	$30 billion	2.33
Sudan	$0.6	$13 billion	4.62
Yugoslavia	$0.5	$12 billion	4.17

* 2000 Funding

Figures are for latest year available, usually 2001. Expenditures are used in a few cases where official budgets are significantly lower than actual spending. The figure for the United States is from the annual budget request for Fiscal Year 2003. Table prepared by Center for Defense Information.

Sources: International Institute for Strategic Studies, Department of Defense, calculations are by the authors.

allowed to have an army, it seems that the country is trying to make up for lost time. On a percentage of GDP basis, the Japanese military is the highest in the industrialized world. This could be one of the reasons why the Japanese economy has been showing "lackluster" performance in recent years.

Exhibit 2.1 also illustrates that Islamic countries, relatively speaking, have much higher military budgets as a percentage of their respective GDPs. It is critical to raise a question regarding this fact. Are they simply belligerent or more concerned about hostility around them? This becomes a critical question, the answer to which may offer a solution to resolve the explosive conditions. Considering that Israel's military budget is nine percent of its GDP, which is higher than any Muslim country except Saudi Arabia, one may conclude that Arab countries are trying to cope with or are intimidated by Israel. In most cases, it appears that the countries that do not have much in terms of wealth and gross national product are spending much money on military preparedness.

Third world countries in general must scale down their militarism in favor of economic advancement. Many of them allocate large proportions of their budgets to the military even though there may not be an obvious external threat except the perception of insecurity and some degree of paranoia. The greed factor is very capable of contributing to these insecurities and resultant paranoia. Certain power groups with the help of some global corporate giants try to achieve more power as the economic conditions become dismal for masses.

There is, however, an important additional factor that enters into the picture. Many third world governments arm themselves against their own people so that they maintain themselves in power. Since many of them are not democracies and are ruled by strong but not very well-liked leaders, an internal power structure is essential for these leaders to remain in power. Such "regime security" practices reduce the chances of democratization of these societies and create additional economic hardship.

However, given the high proportions of illiteracy, it is not clear that democracy can work in these countries. Since democracies thrive on a reasonably rational voting citizenry, illiteracy is a major barrier to the advancement of democracy in third world countries. Thus, it appears that high military expenditures, coupled with or even accelerated by increased military expenditures, present a catch-22. Economic, political, and military stagnations are supported by excessive rates of illiteracy and even further increased by religiosity. Religiosity here is a cause and effect at the same time. As demarcation takes place, religiosity advances. As religiosity advances, demarcation between cultures become more prominent.

As conflicts and wars take place, one must consider the expenditures. In addition to the loss of lives and damage to properties, it is critical to consider that each smart bomb costs one million dollars. It is further necessary to realize that, even in the United States, there are hundreds of thousands of schools that need remodeling, refurbishment, and repair. One million dollars can go a long way in that direction.

In short, accelerating militarism is not likely to be beneficial to anybody with possible exception of a few global corporate giants using globalization as a weapon to increase their economic gains. In reality, all parties lose, and economic development is deterred. Continuation of this militarism can, and quite likely will, lead to destruction of countries and even the world itself. There seems to be a need for an established limit to military preparedness before it destroys us directly by wars or indirectly by deterring economic and educational progresses that are desperately needed.

Illiteracy and Militarism

The fear of the unknown is universal; however, how much fear and what level of understanding should prevail among nations become critical questions. The fear factor can easily be related to a cultural trait which is coined by Hofstede as risk aversion. Hofstede contends that different cultures treat risk differently, and the intensity of the perceived risk is totally different because of differing cultural traits. Accordingly, some societies train their people to beat the future. In those societies, people are more nervous, emotional, and aggressive. If these societies see the risk intensified, they will take strong positions to avoid the risk. Hence, different cultures have different ways of coping with risk but perceptions go to extremes. Here, over and beyond the cultural traits, it is also critical to understand that the perceived risk stems from the unknown as well. This means that the lack of knowledge or ignorance could accelerate the power of perceived risk by the populace.

It is reasonable to be suspicious or even worried about the unknown; however, lack of knowledge can easily force a group or a nation to exaggerate this phenomenon. If the risks seem more imminent and more dangerous, the perception of risk may be broader and more serious. The modern-day surge of militarism appears to be tied into this lack of knowledge and understanding which is a function of illiteracy. If the illiteracy rate is very high, the country may be more concerned about the unknown. Possibly illiteracy-caused lack of knowledge further accelerates the fear of the unknown, which may lead to further militarism.

Exhibit 2.2 presents the illiteracy ranking of the highest military spenders. As can be seen, a number of countries such as United Arab Emirates, Vietnam, Singapore, and Iraq, among many others, show rather high levels of illiteracy commensurate with their military spending. As has been discussed up to this point, illiteracy is rather closely related to the risk of unknown, and, as a result, the risk-evasive activity concentrates on militarism.

A statistical analysis to examine this relationship between illiteracy and militarism has been performed by the authors . Military spending rankings were correlated with illiteracy ranking. The results are presented in Exhibit 2.3. As can be seen, the relationship between the two measures is statistically significant, indicating that indeed many countries with very high military spending experience large-scale illiteracy. Thus the more illiterate a country, the more militaristic it is. Although a correlation analysis such as this one does not show or prove causation between the two phenomena observed, the findings of this analysis are rather alarming. Since many of these countries are allocating large national resources to militaristic activity, they

Exhibit 2.2 Military spending and illiteracy ranking

Country	Military spending	Illiteracy rates
Russia	1	25
Saudi Arabia	2	8
Japan	3	28
Israel	4	20
United Arab Emirates	5	7
Iran	6	11
Kuwait	7	10
North Korea	8	28
Vietnam	9	16
Singapore	10	16
Iraq	11	1
Luxembourg	12	28
Sudan	13	5
Pakistan	14	2
Yugoslavia	15	28
Syria	16	6
United States	17	28
Libya	18	9
Turkey	19	12
Brazil	20	14
China	21	12
India	22	4
Taiwan	23	19
Greece	24	22
South Korea	25	25
Colombia	26	15
United Kingdom	27	28
Cuba	28	22
Egypt	29	3
Poland	30	28
Sweden	31	28
France	32	28
Czech Republic	33	28
Australia	34	28
Norway	35	28
Philippines	36	20
Hungary	37	28
Denmark	38	28
Netherlands	39	28
Italy	40	28
Spain	41	25
Portugal	42	16
Germany	43	28
Argentina	44	22
Canada	45	28
Belgium	46	28

may not have enough resources to educate their populations and, hence, the relationship between militarism and illiteracy becomes a self-fulfilling prophecy.

The greed factor has everything to gain and very little to lose, in the short run, from accelerating militarism and continuing illiteracy. Emphasizing short-run excessive economic power rather than long-run prosperity and understanding for masses cannot be easily stopped and reversed.

Exhibit 2.3 Spearman (rank-ordered) correlation between military spending and illiteracy rates

```
. use "C:\SQDATA\MILILLIT.dta", clear
(Spearman (Rank-ordered) correlation)

. spearman spending literacy

Number of obs =    46
Spearman's rho =     0.4657

Test of Ho: spending and literacy independent
   Pr > | t | =          0.0011
```

The data indicate that higher military spending (% of GDP) is positively correlated with higher illiteracy rates with a probability of almost 99%.

Summary

Globalization, it is maintained here, is thriving primarily on the greed factor making a few extremely rich and powerful, and others insecure and frustrated. Hostilities emerging from these situations are creating more emphasis on military might. International hostilities are giving rise to stronger military–industrial complexes. Military expenditures, it is maintained in this chapter, are proportionate to rates of illiteracy. The lack of mutual trust is interfering with the development of a permanent piece.

References

Brakow, Tom (2000), *The Greatest Generation*, New York: Random House.
Clark, Woodrow W. Jr. (1994), "Defense Conversion," *The Journal of Business and Industrial Marketing*, 9(4): 54–68.
Einstein, Albert (1993), *Einstein on Humanism*, New York: Citadel Press.
Wall, Robert (2004), "Cashing in on Defense: Increased Pentagon Spending Bolsters Company Profits in 2003 and Beyond," *Aviation Week and Space Technology*, February 2, 29–30.

Chapter 3
The Physical Status of the Fragile Planet

It is simply ironic that at this point in time we can destroy the world with all the super nuclear bombs we have, but we have no solution to nuclear, toxic, and human waste problems. The planet is *not* growing, but its population is growing at a very fast pace. As its population grows, its resources deplete and its environment deteriorates. Attaining environmental sustainability and just maintaining a normal quality of life are difficult enough, but adding on to these the cultural clashes and militaristic demarcation that are discussed earlier is clearly leading the fragile planet that we live in into very questionable state of survival and continuity.

The United States, for instance, is accountable for only about four percent of the world's population and is responsible for about 25 percent of the toxic and environmentally questionable emissions. Here the role of industrialized and fast-industrializing countries' actions must be questioned. When Country A is polluting and Country B is trying to cut down its environmentally destructive emissions, the end result is just the same. Both countries are, sooner or later, going to feel the negative influences and experience the outcomes of pollution. The small and fragile planet cannot do anything about it unless the players recognize the problem and modify their behavior patterns and the value systems that are directing these destructive forces.

Three issues are particularly important when the physical status of the world is considered: First, the human economy is a dependent subset of the biosphere. However, this is not quite understood and internalized by different countries. In general, some economists believe that environmental quality is most effectively achieved through market forces and, hence, does not need any kind of management. Second, environmental sustainability must be attained. But it does not come automatically, and such sustainability can be achieved only by a major effort among disciplines and not just economics. Third, although for human populations, sustainability means transforming consumption behaviors in such a way that the ecosystems will not be overly taxed, there is no collective vision worldwide as to how to attain sustainability. In fact, a very important influence of the greed factor is that short-run profits are more important than long-term sustainability.

Existing societies, governments, and particularly businesses do not incorporate adequate thinking which reflects significant appreciation of environmental

A.C. Samli, *Globalization from the Bottom Up*,
DOI: 10.1007/978-0-387-77098-7_3, © Springer Science+Business Media, LLC 2008

criticalities and the key elements of sustainability of the physical status of the fragile planet (McMichael, Butler and Folke 2003).

Pollution and the Future

The fragile planet is physically smaller than ever before in terms of moving goods and services, moving technology, moving know-how, moving capital, and moving information. Particularly the Internet is extremely active in making the world smaller by improving the speed of communications worldwide.

Lester R. Brown (2004) states: "The world is moving into uncharted territory as human demands override the sustainable yield of natural systems." He goes on to say that "we lived off the interest generated by the Earth's natural capital assets but we are now consuming those assets. We have built an environmental bubble economy." He posits that the bubble could burst if nothing is done about it. The bubble is artificially inflated and cannot continue.

A team of scientists estimated that humanity's collective demands first surpassed the Earth's regenerative capacity in 1980. By 1999 our demands were estimated to exceed the Earth's capacity by 20 percent (Brown 2004). If these facts are close to reality, we all are living on borrowed time. Here demand for fresh water, clean air, clean energy, and arable clean soil is increasing geometrically and creating a nightmare for the scientific community that is particularly concerned about these issues.

During the last half of the 20th century, human population grew more than it did during four million years preceding that period. More specifically, as the world population doubled during the last half century, the global economy expanded seven-fold. Thus, the fragile planet is asked to give more than it can possibly give (Brown 2004).

Increasing pollution is due to the fact that trees are cut before they can regenerate, range lands are overgrazed, erosions in cropland are exceeding new soil formation, fish are taken from the ocean faster than they can reproduce, nonrenewable fossil fuels are depleted, and carbon dioxide (CO_2) is released faster than nature can absorb it. It has been stated that rising atmospheric CO_2 levels are raising the Earth's temperature (Brown 2004).

The result of increasing pollution is named the *mega-threat*, which is the planet's climate change. This threat will create intense heat waves, destructive storms, lower crop yields, glacier melting, and rising seas. In other words, it will make the fragile planet uninhabitable.

Lack of Controls Means Bleak Future

Although there are many well-meaning organizations in North America and Europe, who may be trying to reverse the prevailing dismal picture, the problem cannot be solved by piecemeal efforts. Since there is neither a global agreement nor an authority to administer the clauses in such an agreement, there can be no progress by the fragile planet except for conditions to become worse. Cleaning the air and pursuing an environmentally responsible overall policy, for instance, in Sweden will do nothing about the environmental abuse by India, China, or the United States. The fragile planet is not growing or cannot be treated in an isolated manner by countries or regions that are practicing extremely different policies toward the environment knowingly or unknowingly. After all, if Mexico pollutes and California is trying to clean the air, just what is going to be accomplished? These two places are not from different planets. If their efforts offset each other, there still will be no progress. Without some serious global authority, there can be no progress. If the estimates of the scientific community are correct, without such an authority, the fragile planet appears to be virtually doomed.

Environmental Responsibility Is Everybody's Business

Brown (2004, p. 97) posits that "unless we respond to social and environmental issues undermining our future, we may not be able to avoid economic decline and social disintegration." Here "we" is not just one group or one nation, it is all of us, the whole global community. With all the culture clash, ethnic strife, and militarism, how can the world community get together and make decisions regarding the future of our world?

Attaining environmental sustainability means maximizing the chances that environmental and social conditions will indefinitely support human security, well-being, and health. This requires not only transforming our way of living, but making sure that disciplines dealing with human conditioning, i.e., demography, economics, ecology, and epidemiology, are all in cooperation. Finally, not a few but all countries must agree and participate in efforts to attain sustainability (McMichael, Butler and Folke 2003). But none of this is happening at this point in time.

Instead of acting in unison, countries are still going in their own chosen direction. Only 36 countries out of almost 200, mostly in Europe and Japan, have basically stabilized their populations. At least these countries can provide proper economic and social conditions for their respective populations; however, if the rest of the nations do not have the same orientation and do not act accordingly, there does not seem to be much hope for the fragile planet (Brown 2004).

As populations increase uncontrollably, in addition to the air pollution, water tables are falling and soil is eroding. Water tables are falling because of excessive use. Failure to stop the fall in water tables is likely to lead to an abrupt cut-back in water supplies with dramatic impacts on food production and normal quality of life (Brown 2004).

Soil erosion, despite the individual efforts of certain countries such as the United States and South Korea, is an extremely critical environmental problem since continuing soil loss is not matched by soil formation. Partial and temporary retirement of most erodible croplands and developing no-till and other soil conservation practices are not at all common practice throughout the world (Brown 2004). Thus, environmental responsibility, particularly the lack thereof, is everybody's business and must be understood and treated as such. There is no such orientation in the world at this point in time.

In Chapter 1 we discussed the greed versus the ambition factors. Particularly in environmental issues, the greed factor is very present and has tremendously damaging and dangerous implications. The following four examples are simply an illustration of a very long and continuing list of offensive activities to the environment of the fragile planet.

Exxon Valdez is perhaps one of the most offensive incidents in environmental happenings. A tremendous oil spill in Alaska left a very damaging aftermath. Exxon paid a little sum as penalty and claimed that the damage had been taken care of.

Union Carbide built a factory in Bhopal, India. Unfortunately, in the hands of untrained Indian workers, the plant had a tremendous explosion injuring some 30,000 people.

When it was found out that asbestos causes asbestosis, a disabling if not deadly disease, instead of discontinuing its production, asbestos production moved to India where there are no laws against its production.

Nuclear power has caused tremendous amounts of atmospheric pollution that is not only killing people but creating a large variety of birth defects. Unfortunately this is not the extent of the damage nuclear energy production is capable of. Nuclear waste is estimated to last about 100,000 years, and if there is enough of it generated, it could easily destroy the world.

These are only a few examples of a very critical problem that is driven by greed. Companies that are involved in such extensive pollution activity have not been forced to undo the damage they have caused. In many cases, the damage that has been caused cannot possibly be reversed.

One of the most controversial environment-related topics in recent years is global warming. Unchecked, this development could cause flooding, ocean disruptions, shifting storm patterns, reduced farm output, animal extinction, and droughts, among other devastating effects (Carey 2004).

Power Structures Versus Environmental Needs

Display of power by the central authorities, democratic or despotic, is almost essential to maintain a leadership position within a country and protect the country against outside hostilities. This reinforcement of authority and central power that may lead in the reelection of the key players in democracies and extend the existing power base in autocracies usually has nothing to do with environmentalism and environment-friendly attitudes. In fact, when the central authority in the country wants to display power to threaten its enemies and gain the respect of the country's population and hence builds nuclear weapons and tests them, the environmental damage caused cannot be justified easily. Even if it is justified, the damage cannot be reversed.

Whereas it may be impressive to the population if the central government is accumulating weapons of mass destruction and starting politically visible and desirable but environmentally detrimental heavy industries, the conflicts between the existing power structure and environmental needs become clear.

Existing power structures, by definition, try to maintain their power base. Such a power base cannot be maintained by saying "sissy" environmentalism as opposed to "powerful" industrialism or militarism. Thus the fragile planet faces a very questionable future.

The Throwaway Economy Versus Eco-economy

Our discussion thus far in this book illustrates that this world is under the influence of what may be coined a "throwaway" economy. This economy is ruled by power structures, militarism, and the "greed" factor. This economy pollutes, disrupts, and creates total imbalance between the haves and have-nots. It is based on the use of fossil fuels and creates much economic power by overemphasizing waste (Brown 2002). The market forces that are ruling today's global economy are based on the above-mentioned "throwaway" economy. In such an economy, two powerful forces are in effect. They are coined here the *greed factor* and the *need factor*. While the greed factor has no limits, no boundaries, and practically no scruples, the need factor basically can be satisfiable. The hierarchy model that is attributed to Maslow indicates, for instance, that most essential physiological needs, safety needs, and the rest of the hierarchy are all manageable with reasonable limitations (Kotler 2002). But perhaps starting with the top of the hierarchy needs, and beyond, there are no boundaries. As basic needs of third world countries or the poor in general are at least partially taken care of, tremendous profits are realized by the companies that are taking short cuts and not facilitating the ecological needs. In short, the companies that are addressing some of the needs prevailing in emerging countries are not paying attention to the environment. In fact, they are polluting the environment irresponsibly. However, those who are providing the goods and services have followed and are following the greed factor. Obscene profits are realized, equally obscene salaries are paid, and Earth's resources are challenged. There are, once again, no authorities to check and control the practices of the throwaway economy. Particularly, dealing with global economic conditions, international giants are making tremendous profits in the absence of any controlling or directing authority without any payback to the environment, as if there is no tomorrow.

The eco-economy, as defined by Brown (2002), "is one that satisfies today's needs without jeopardizing the prospects of future generations to meet theirs." Brown goes further to articulate that such an economy would consider the key role of photosynthesis, would emphasize sustainable yield, would pay attention to nutrient cycles, and would make provision for the sensitive role of climate, among others. A sustainable eco-economy has to make sure that in all aspects of production the demands from the environment will not exceed the sustainable yield. As long as the harvest does not exceed the sustainable yield, the fragile planet will continue its survival (Brown 2002). It is reasonable to posit that the need factor can be consistent with the eco-economy requirements; however, the greed factor goes way beyond these requirements. At this point in time, there does not seem to be major activity trying to instate (unfortunately not reinstate) a sustainable eco-economy. In fact, the greed factor is such that the throwaway economy that is ruled by the greed factor has been reporting to *dishonest accounting systems*.

The Dishonest Accounting Systems

Every product produced in our societies has a cost. This cost can easily be broken into private and public components. Whereas we have developed very sophisticated cost accounting systems for private costs, we have done almost nothing for public costs (Samli 2000). In other words, we can calculate the cost of production of a product without accounting for environmental damage or waste it will create. This is equal to treating all products as being ecologically safe or neutral. It is not only that not enough attention has been paid to the social or public cost of the product, but there has not been adequate effort to calculate such a cost. The methodology is not advanced and, at the point of writing this book, little if any activity is taking place in this area. The challenge of creating an "honest market" that would calculate the value of nature's services is not met. If the total private and public costs are calculated, the total cost can be incorporated within the market price. Such an activity would enable restructuring of the tax system in such a way that environmentally destructive activities will be taxed accordingly and, hence, the tax structure will force manufacturers to pay more attention to the ecological aspects of all products and services. In Brown's words (2004, p. 95): "...a tax on coal would incorporate the increased health care costs associated with breathing polluted air, the costs of damage from acid rain and the costs of climate disruption."

In addition to not calculating or accounting for environmental costs each year, the taxpayers of the world underwrite $700 billion in subsidies for activities that are environmentally destructive. This would include burning fossil fuels, overfishing, overpumping oil and water, or cutting forests, among others (Brown 2004). Thus, not only is environmental responsibility not present, but paying for environmental irresponsibility may be on the rise. An Earth Council study entitled *Subsidizing Unsustainable Development* observes, "There is something unbelievable about the world spending hundreds of billions of dollars annually to subsidize its own destruction" (Brown 2004, p. 96). The situation is quite likely worsening rather than getting better.

In Chapter 2 it is shown that military expenditures correlate with illiteracy. It is also hypothesized here that the military spending and environmental offensiveness also correlate. In terms of the pollution of air and water, it appears that the most industrialized countries are the major offenders. However, a rank correlation between air and water pollution and military expenditures does not show a relationship between pollution and military expenditures for less-developed countries. This is because they are not industrialized enough to pollute the air and the water

(Exhibit 3.1). These countries mostly buy the military supplies from the industrialized countries. Although these countries spend enough on military supplies, they buy them rather than produce them. Thus they do not directly contribute to the pollution, but they spend more than what would be the educational and health-related sums that are needed to move these societies forward. Furthermore, by demanding

Exhibit 3.1 Air and water pollution ranking of major military spenders

Country	A+W rank	Air rank	Water rank
Australia	1	5	8
Norway	2	18	3
Canada	3	6	16
Libya	4	21	3
Denmark	5	15	11
Greece	6	22	6
United Arab Emirates	7	1	28
Belgium	7	10	19
Israel	9	11	19
Kuwait	9	2	28
Netherlands	9	19	11
Russia	12	12	19
United States	12	3	28
Argentina	14	32	3
Syria	15	34	2
Cuba	16	37	1
Saudi Arabia	17	8	34
Poland	17	23	19
Czech Republic	19	9	34
United Kingdom	20	16	28
Spain	20	25	19
Hungary	22	29	16
Iran	23	31	16
Colombia	23	41	6
Brazil	25	40	8
Singapore	26	7	42
Sweden	26	30	19
India	28	42	8
Egupt	28	39	11
Japan	30	17	34
Yogoslavia	31	33	19
Germany	32	13	40
Iraq	33	35	19
Taiwan	33	26	28
Philippines	33	43	11
Pakistan	36	44	11
Turkey	36	36	19
France	36	27	28
North Korea	39	20	40
Portugal	40	28	34
Italy	41	24	39
China	42	37	34

Source: Based on World Bank Human Development Reports (2003). A+W rankings are by the authors.

sophisticated military supplies, they contribute indirectly to the on-going pollution in the fragile planet.

If the Planet Does Not Survive, No One Can

Environmentally, the fragile planet appears to be totally stressed out. Its future is rather questionable. It is critical to realize that individual countries such as Belgium, France, Germany, or Japan may be individually trying to counteract these rather discouraging patterns. However, the individual efforts are not likely to make a dent, since most other countries are not joining in and considering the environmental threats as seriously as they should be considered. For less-developed and lesser-educated countries, environmental considerations may be considered some kind of a "sissy" activity as opposed to the "macho" activity of militarism. The greatest danger lies in the fact that it is not understood that piecemeal efforts in this all-out survival issue cannot be effective enough. Somehow polluters are not acknowledging that if the fragile planet cannot survive, no one can. Above everything else, the well-being and environmental health of the planet Earth has to be considered, and all efforts must be made to create and maintain a sustainable eco-economy.

One of the most significant efforts in constructing an environmental blueprint was undertaken by the International Chamber of Commerce that is based in Paris. The Chamber attempted to place environmental management issues very high in corporate agendas. The outcome of this effort is a 16-point plan of action that may be considered as the most profound statement for environmental protection. A summary of this 16-point plan is presented in Exhibit 3.2.

Exhibit 3.2 The proposed environment protection plan

- Environmental management is one of the highest corporate priorities
- Environmental policies and practices are a key element of management
- Business' environmental performance must improve
- Educate and motivate employees in environmental protection management
- All new projects must be assessed in terms of their environmental impact
- New products and services must not harm the environment
- All customers must be advised how to use products safely
- Facilities and activities must be managed in an energy-efficient manner
- Conduct environment protection-related research
- Use products or services that do not create environmental damage
- All the contractors and functionaries of companies must use these principles
- Develop emergency preparedness plans
- Transfer technologies to environmental soundness
- Support public policies to enhance environmental protection
- Educate the public regarding potential hazards of not paying attention to environmental protection
- Evaluate environmental performances by regular environmental audits

Source: Adapted and revised from Ember (2001).

What About Population Increase

Many years ago Julian Huxley made the following observation (1960, p. 81):

> Everything points to one conclusion. While every effort must be made to increase food production to facilitate distribution, to conserve all conservable resources to shame the "have" nations into a fairer sharing of the good things of the world with the "have-nots," this alone cannot prevent disaster. Birth control also is necessary, on a world scale and as soon as possible.

More than 50 years have passed since these words were uttered; however, if anything, the world's population is increasing at an accelerated rate. Without thinking about industrial and military pollution, one can easily conclude that sheer population explosion creates tremendous hardship for the fragile planet. Just as is true in all restaurants or public meeting places, the world also has limited space and can support only so many people. Each person pollutes a little bit, which is compounded by the billions of people. With population explosion along with military and industrial pollution, the whole problem of survivability of the fragile planet is exacerbated. There seems to be no relief in sight. In Friedman's words (2000, p. 302), "...without environment there is no sustainable culture and without a sustainable culture there is no sustainable community and without a sustainable community there is no sustainable globalization."

The environmental fears have been categorized in five groups: diminishing natural resources, ever-growing population, forests are disappearing, air and water are becoming more polluted, and global warming is a reality (Lomborg 2001). Although all of these five groups are a reality, some analysts maintain that they are not progressing as rapidly as estimated by environmentalists earlier and, indeed, there is still time to reverse these trends. In other words, there is still some optimism. However, temporary submissions in these trends mean only postponement. Unless a concerted effort is made to reverse these trends, sooner or later the fragile planet will self-destruct. Thus, environmental responsibility on the part of industries and companies is a must. Despite Lomborg's (2001) optimism that the market system can cope with these problems, the authors believe that this is an extremely risky proposition and, if it is wrong, there will be no turning back.

Of these five environmental threats, global warming is becoming the most pressing issue. There is a consensus that we must combat this factor causing climatic changes. If nothing is done about it, global warming is going to cause flooding, ocean disruptions, shifts in storm patterns, reduction in farm output, extinction of some animal species, and fertile areas becoming barren and dry (Carey 2004). Although there is much discussion about this threat, there is no general agreement as to how it should be counteracted.

Summary

This chapter is emphasizing the fact that the world is a very fragile planet and it is in grave danger. There is no global consensus to not to overtax the ecosystems. The demand for fresh water, clean energy, and arable clean soil is increasing geometrically and there is no relief in sight. Environmental responsibility, although should be everybody's concern, is not at all paid attention to. The chapter connects the discouraging physical status on the planet to the greed factor that is articulated in Chapter 1. Furthermore, the runaway world population increase is making the situation almost totally hopeless. However, the chapter presents an environmental protection plan which can make a major contribution.

References

Brown, Lester R. (2004), *Mother Earth News*, April/May.
Brown, Lester R. (2002), "Planning For the Eco-Economy (Ecology)," *USA Today Magazine*, March.
Carey, John (2004), "Global Warming," *Business Week*, August 16, 60–69.
Ember, Lois (2001), "Environment Protection," *Chemical and Engineering News*, April 8, 4.
Friedman, Thomas L. (2000), *The Lexus and The Olive Tree*, New York: Achor Books.
Kotler, Philip (2002), *Marketing Management*, Upper Saddle River, NJ: Prentice Hall.
Lomborg, Bjorn (2001), "The Truth About the Environment," in *Globalisation*, 232–238, London: The Economist.
Malthus, Thomas, Huxley, Julian, and Osborn, Frederick (1960), *Three Essays On Population*, New York: Mentor Books.
McMichael, Anthony C., Butler, C. D., Folke, Carl (2003), "New Visions for Addressing Sustainability," *Science*, December 12, 1919–1925.
Samli, A. Coskun (2000), *Empowering The American Consumer*, Westport, CT: Quorum Books.

Chapter 4
The Most Promising Tool is Partly the Cause

- World Space plans to reach 200 million households in the world's emerging markets by direct broadcast satellite.
- NSamara will use three satellites to bring direct-to-person digital audio broadcasting to many third world markets by using digital, portable, small receivers.
- Grameen-Phone markets cell phones to 35,000 villages in Bangladesh by hiring village women as agents who lease phone time to other villagers, one call at a time.
- Colgate-Palmolive rolls into Indian villages with video vans that show the benefit of toothbrushing and expected to earn over half of its Indian revenue from rural areas by 2003.
- An Indian-Australian car manufacturer created an affordable rural transport vehicle to compete with "bullock carts" rather than cars. The vehicle functions well at low speeds and carries up to two tons.
- Fiat developed a "third world car," the Palio that far outsells the Ford Fiesta in Brazil and that will be launched in other developing nations.
- Corporacion GEO builds low-income housing in Mexico. The two-bedroom homes are modular and can be expanded as owners increase their income. The company is now expanding into Chile and poor southern U.S. communities.
- A Latin-American building-supply retailer offers bags of cement in small sizes to customers building their own homes.
- Pillsbury is trying to enter the Indian market with products such as microwaveable pizza.

These are typical examples of far-reaching impact of globalization. Throughout written history, there has never been a tool such as globalization that could enhance the economic performance of all countries and particularly help the emerging countries to accelerate their economic progress. However, as it stands, globalization, almost by definition, is appealing primarily to the upper class in emerging markets. Only a small proportion, if any, is trickling down to locals, spreading the wealth, and improving the quality of life of the locals who are very poor.

A.C. Samli, *Globalization from the Bottom Up*,
DOI: 10.1007/978-0-387-77098-7_4, © Springer Science+Business Media, LLC 2008

If we were to encapsulate what appears to be the insurmountable problem of the fragile planet, we may say the industrialized countries are worried about losing what they have, and developing countries are frustrated because they are not even close to the status of the industrialized world. In fact, they are getting further behind as the world's trade and industrial activities continue as they are (Samli 2004).

If there were to be a bridge between the two distinct parts of the planet, that would be globalization. Globalization, that is, the elimination of barriers to flows of international capital, information, technology and know-how, is the last vestige of hope to enhance understanding, communication, and particularly the economic gap between the two human poles of the fragile planet – the haves and have-nots.

Globalization, if used effectively, can easily bridge the gap between the industrialized world and the third world. This would mean better communication, more understanding, and deemphasizing militarism on the part of world communities. However, as discussed in the previous three chapters, this is not likely to happen all by itself. In fact, if left alone, the adverse conditions created by total globalization not only are threatening the world but are most likely to get worse.

As Stiglitz (2002, p. 9) states

Fundamentally, globalization is the closer integration of the countries and peoples of the world which has been brought about by the enormous reduction of costs of transportation and communication, and the breaking down of artificial barriers to the flows of goods, services, capital, knowledge (and to a lesser extent) people across borders.

As the above quotation indicates, in the history of mankind, there never has been a greater opportunity to spread out not necessarily wealth but wealth-creating capabilities that should not only bridge the gap between haves and have-nots but also create the atmosphere for both parties to join forces for mutual advantage.

As mentioned earlier, the four flows that are the crux of globalization cannot be achieved by a developing country all by itself. Exhibit 4.1 illustrates these four flows.

Capital Flow

Foreign direct investments (FDIs) have become and are a rather routine activity. Many multinational corporations have numerous plants throughout the world. Some of these investments are made in the third world for various reasons. In theory, they can be very useful in the receiving countries' economic development; however, as will be seen later in this chapter, this is not materializing. Foreign direct investments are taking out more than what they put into the economy.

Information

At no time in history has information flown faster and reached further. There is a tremendous amount of information made available to all comers for all purposes. Much of the information can be used very effectively for industrialization, for technology development, and primarily for generating consumer value. However, the

Exhibit 4.1 The four flows of globalization

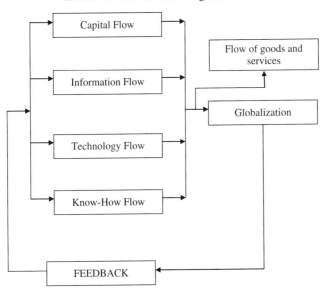

available information is not used as adequately as it could be for the development of third world economies. It is used more readily by those who are already ahead of others, and their use of the information widens the gap between haves and have-nots.

Technology

Technology, defined here as the application of science to economic problems, is the most critical element of globalization. Many third world countries, because of the technologies they imported from advanced countries, have developed their economies. These newly industrialized countries (NICs) such as Singapore, South Korea, Hong Kong, and Taiwan have imported technologies. They have made these technologies operational and produced many products, components, parts, and the like and sold them in global markets. Such activity made a significant and positive difference in their efforts to become more economically well off. The so-called "four tigers of Asia" moved rapidly from the status of have-not to having much more than the average third world country. In all four, there was and is a very active intelligentsia that considers the country's economic growth along with its own economic gain. It is necessary to realize that unless the technology is transferred, the recipient may never be able to develop its technology. If Samsung and Emerson, two major South Korean companies, did not receive the technologies from Japan and produce for Japanese companies for many years, it is doubtful they could have developed the electronic product technologies that they successfully transferred on their own.

Without proper conditions such as qualified personnel, special skills, proper infrastructure, and the like, the technology cannot be successfully transferred. Without these conditions and without the proper technology to be transferred, it would have taken decades more for the Korean companies to develop the technology, if at all.

Know-How

Generating information, utilizing capital investments properly, and transferring technology are all dependent on adequate human resources that can make all these happen. In the globalization process of the past two decades, executive and consulting know-hows have been flowing from one country to another internationally. Thus, the human resource shortage is partially remedied so that globalization can continue.

The four flows are made possible because of decentralization, deregulation, privatization, and the development of cyberspace. These four antecedents have been taking place in all parts of the world but not necessarily at the same level of intensity (Samli 2004). These four necessary but not sufficient conditions of globalization and the four flows of globalization present an unprecedented opportunity for the emerging world countries. The sufficient condition is benefiting all through globalization by making its features reach out to all not to just a few select people. If there were any possibilities for the less-developed parts of the world to become more developed and, hence, to bridge the gap between the rich and the poor, this would be a most desirable goal. However, first the preceding conditions required for globalization are not of the same level of development in various parts of the world. If, for instance, privatization is more developed in country A as opposed to country B, then the impact of the four flows of globalization may be quite different in these two countries.

Second, the utilization of the globalization flows is not quite the same in all poor countries. As seen in the above example of the four Asian tigers, some countries can benefit incomparably more from the globalization process than others.

Third and most importantly, the four flows of globalization do not flow evenly to various countries. In fact, just the opposite is happening. While they might be making significant contributions in one country, or mostly some regions of one country, their impact is not good enough in another.

Capital flow is going only to places where there would be an immediate pay off. Hence, many companies are choosing their target locations very selectively. Thus, foreign direct investments (FDIs) are targeted very selectively and hence they are benefiting just a few select locations.

Information flow has two components: (1) The prospective recipients of information flow must have the capability to receive the information. Here, some countries and some regions are more capable of receiving information because technologically, scientifically, and linguistically there are no barriers to the flow. (2) The information received must be put to work. Certainly, some receivers are more prone to utilizing the information received immediately and effectively. Again, the impact of information flow is extremely variable and, hence, it can be strictly a boon or bane.

Technology flow has even more prerequisites. There are multiple barriers to technology flow, varying from cultural barriers to infrastructural barriers (Samli 1985). Successful technology transfer implies overcoming these barriers successfully. Again, as seen in the case of the four Asian tigers, choosing the right technology and transferring it successfully is not only different but also extremely critical in terms of the receiving country's economic future. The four tigers managed to choose the most appropriate as well as most adequate technologies for their needs. But, all third world countries are not so lucky or so shrewd.

Finally, the know-how flow, whether encouraged by foreign direct investments in technology transfer activity, is simply not quite adequately distributed, meaning that for whatever reason, some countries, companies, or regions receive more of the know-how flow. Similarly, while some countries, companies, or regions are getting great benefits from the know-how flow, others are totally left out of it. The know-how flow, by definition, enables the recipients to choose better industries, to manage them well, make proper investments when needed, and many other critical management decisions that are necessary for economic growth.

As can be seen from our discussion thus far, globalization is an extremely powerful process that offers an escape mechanism from the vicious cycle of economic underdevelopment (Samli 1985). If used properly, the tools of globalization and all the conditions that are required for the emergence of globalization are perhaps the only select few outlets for the less-developed countries. If effective globalization were to exist and countries were to successfully participate in it, then all of the problems that are discussed in the first three chapters of this book could be resolved holistically. However, using Friedman's (2000) definition of globalization as "Darwinism on steroids" tells the whole story. Globalization is simply taking over the industrial activity in a sweeping manner and benefiting primarily a few privileged groups in the third world.

Thus, globalization, what may be the last opportunity for those who are identified as have-nots to develop their economies, is not working in the right direction. It is actually worsening the situation. Thus, the most promising tool to solve many of the problems discussed so far is becoming more of a cause than the solution.

The author developed a balance sheet indicating the assets and liabilities of globalization. Exhibit 4.2 illustrates both sides of globalization. Information presented in the exhibit is not exhaustive. Only some of the most important aspects of globalization are listed. Both assets and liabilities presented in Exhibit 4.2 are reasonably self-explanatory. Some of the finer points of Exhibit 4.2 are further depicted in Exhibit 4.3. On the assets column, the key points are all based on Exhibit 4.1. All four flows, i.e., information, technology, know-how, and capital, create the many positive aspects of globalization. These positive aspects indicate why globalization can be a spectacular vehicle to bridge the gap between the emerging countries and industrialized countries. In the liability column, some of the problems that are discussed in the first three chapters of this book are presented in greater detail. Perhaps the following statement depicts the picture well: "Globalization is a great

Exhibit 4.2 A balance sheet of globalization

Assets	Liabilities
1. Simplification and facilitation of the movement from command to demand economies. Help for emerging countries	1. Possibility of big companies exploiting small countries, winner take all
2. Facilitation of the technology and intellectual capital flow transfer, most powerful asset	2. Creation of global oligopolies, leaving millions of consumers behind
3. The emergence of Newly Industrialized Countries (NICs) due to technology transfer and trade	3. Information technology can develop a superpower of its own through globalization, giving unfair advantage to use IT
4. Increase in accessibility to global markets, emerging countries can participate in world trade	4. Globalization goes beyond the existing legal boundaries, weakening of geographic boundaries
5. Improvement of consumers' well-being around the world, more information for better decisions	5. Creation of very high paying jobs in certain industries and unemployment in many others, creating a strong dichotomy
6. Facilitation of freer trade, increasing the volume of trade	6. Rules of the game are not established; there are no authorities to mediate unfair practices
7. Facilitation of free flow of raw materials, semifinished products, i.e., sourcing, again increasing the volume of trade	7. Creation of marginalism on the part of small and weak countries, weaker countries are becoming weaker yet
8. Stimulation of a major flow of managerial know-how, opportunity to run companies better	8. Deterioration of the development of local industries, local industries cannot cope with extreme modernities
9. Stimulation of international cooperation and competition in favor of consumers, better opportunities for consumers	9. Creation of extreme discrepancies in global wages, global wages go to a small group of well to do
10. Stimulation of intercultural communication and understanding, better information for everyone	10. Creation of extreme environmental abuse that would not have occurred otherwise. Globalization does not have environmental boundaries
11. Possibility of technological help to enhance the infrastructure development throughout the world, developing the foundation of economic growth	11. Encouragement of the development of a major world market at the risk of ignoring the local markets, local markets lose more power and become ineffective

force for good. But neither governments nor businesses can be trusted to make the case" (*Globalization*, 2001, p. 5).

The author believes the difference between the two columns of globalization is in the difference between the greed factor and the ambition factor. Could these two be

Exhibit 4.3 Globalization's impact on quality of life in the third world

The impact	Outcome	QOL implications*
Big companies are gaining much power	Small companies are pushed out of existence	Small entrepreneurs are losing and oligopolists are gaining
Emerging global oligopolies	Emphasizing mainly small rich markets, ignoring the masses in most parts of the world	Only a select few in the third world are benefiting in the third world at the expense of others
Information technology is used selectively	It enhances the market power of those who are already extremely powerful	The emerging power is used negatively in the winner takes all style
Emphasizing capital-intensive rather than labor-intensive activity	Sending upscale jobs selectively to third world countries	Creating a bigger gap between rich and the poor everywhere
Newly created capitalism power is ignoring local political and cultural entities	Local governments are losing power, and local cultures are threatened	An emerging identity crisis is creating confusion
Environmental irresponsibility expands in favor of short-run profits	An acceleration in environmental assault around the world	Creating a negative impact not only in immediate QOL but also in the future of the world as well
Multinational companies are emerging and growing at the expense of local firms	Small entrepreneurial local firms are not being encouraged to participate in the globalization activity	People are working hard but not receiving good compensation
Benefits are accruing for those who are already rich	Much economic power is accumulating in the hands of a few	Class wars are resulting from hopelessness
The gap between the rich and the poor is widening	If left alone, along with class wars, there will be an accelerated international terrorism	The lack of economic progress is creating negative QOL and political restlessness

QOL = quality of life
Source: Adapted and revised from Samli (2004).

administered in such a way that ambition takes over and the greed factor slowly but surely disappears? Perhaps a way of accomplishing this is the means of promising the fragile planet much hope. The proposition of helping the ambition factor to take a dominant position may be the foundation of social capitalism.

Companies Are Growing Larger than Nations

Stiglitz (2002, p. 214) states, "Globalization today is not working for many of world's poor. It is not working for the environment. It is not working for the stability of the globaleconomy." However shocking it may be, today of the 100 largest economies in the world, 51 are corporations and only 49 are different nation states. It has been estimated that the sales of General Motors and Ford are greater than the GDP of total sub-Saharan states of Africa. Wal-Mart has total sales higher than the revenues of most of the states of Eastern Europe. Today's globalization, unchecked, is likely to continue in the same direction (Hertz 2001). This situation explains the conditions that create one of the all-encompassing themes of this book: macro-problems in the world are being micromanaged. Global giants are not particularly interested in the economic development of the markets they are dealing with per se, unless lack of economic development interferes with their profit picture. And at that point, the company tries to micromanage the situation. This micromanagement practice is not likely to be very beneficial for the economy as a whole, and it causes more harm than good globally.

There is basically nothing wrong with being a global giant corporation except such companies are basically forced to go to most profitable markets and as such, they ignore the majority of the world's population who live in third world countries. Furthermore, they are capable of making decisions that may be very favorable for the company and may go against the best interest of the country.

Global Giants Go Only After Profitable Markets

The total size of emerging world markets combined is greater than the North American and European markets combined (Samli 2004). This means there are great opportunities in these countries that are ignored. Thus, there are billions of people, the forgotten majority, who are left behind. As globalization benefits lucky and privileged small groups, the forgotten majority is either totally left out or the benefits of globalization simply trickle down to these groups in negligible proportions. The major problem with global giants is that they must achieve a large critical sales volume to survive. Pillsbury in India, for instance, is trying to do just that. However, this is a very serious problem, since the markets that are composed of the forgotten majority are extremely diverse. Diversity in terms of needs, locations, tastes, and the like make it extremely difficult and equally unattractive for global giants to cultivate these niche markets.

International giants who are primarily responsible for globalization have certain obvious preferences. First and foremost, they enter world markets from the upper end. That is, they try to enter the best markets. Second, they have to achieve a critical mass, which is not quite possible in the remote rural corners of the emerging world markets. Third, because of their excessive costs, they cannot cater to many small variable markets that are scattered all over the emerging countries. Fourth, to a certain extent, global giants lack flexibility that will empower them to work with the varying needs of the small and local markets of the emerging countries. But above all, they have the option of making good money in the higher echelons of the emerging markets; global giants will see no reason to enter the lower end of these markets (more on this topic in Chapter 6). This is what the author calls top-down globalization (Samli 2004) that appears in select parts of the world and benefits a few select minorities.

If, on the other hand, small, flexible entrepreneurial firms were to enter into these markets from the lower end, they would be able to reach out to the forgotten majority and provide certain specific goods and services that global giants cannot profitably provide.

The one-size-fits-all approach of many global giants does not do the job (Samli 2004). As a result, global giants prefer to go to world markets where the critical sales volume can be achieved with one-size-fits-all products. This approach, by definition, leaves much of the have-not countries out of trade activities of the global giants.

As mentioned earlier, global giants are not quite flexible enough to cater to the varying needs of many smaller world markets composed of the poorer countries. They also lack creativity, since they are almost, by definition, forced to concentrate on one-size-fits-all orientation in major world markets. Economically and managerially, they do not show the flexibility that is needed to survive or to be successful in diverse, smaller markets. Finally, global giants are so far removed from consumers that not only are they not sensitive to consumer needs but they are also not very passionate about satisfying them (Samli 2004).

Global Giants Do Not Create Jobs

Perhaps it is somewhat unfortunate when the global giants are emerging in foreign direct investments (FDIs); they not only make a lot of money, but also eliminate traditional labor-intensive jobs in favor of automation. They do not get engaged in remedying the situation. Furthermore, most of the profits generated by FDIs are not invested in the country but are taken out in large sums. This situation in the long run creates nothing but hardship in the lower layers of the world's economic pyramid.

Our discussion here should not be understood as indicating that globalization is not good for the general well-being of the fragile planet. In fact, on the contrary, the Asian four tigers would not have come into being without globalization. However, globalization, unchecked and uncontrolled, is also creating much hardship throughout the world by making haves, have-mores, have-nots, and have-nothings. Many scholars agree that in its current form, globalization cannot be sustained (Samli 2002). However, as discussed later on in Chapters 6 and 7, a bottom-up globalization as opposed to the current top-down globalization can create a balance and, hence, globalization, top-down and bottom-up together, can benefit the whole world.

Capitalism Takes Many Forms

The reason why the most promising tool, i.e., globalization, is partly the cause of the problems of the fragile planet is that in the 21st century, globalization is based on what is coined earlier, the greed-driven laissez-faire capitalism, but it is a further extended version of it. By definition, laissez-faire capitalism favors the big and the powerful in the marketplace. If there are no rules or conditions to level the playing field, Darwinism on steroids will encourage the use of the greed factor and will play havoc with the existing, and admittedly not very efficient, prevailing market systems of emerging countries. If Darwinism on steroids is further reinforced by the greed factor, as presented in Chapter 1, there appears to be a set of very unfortunate results in the making.

Exhibit 4.3 illustrates some of the most noticeable impacts of globalization on the quality of life (QOL) prevailing in remote parts of the fragile planet. As seen in the exhibit, globalization based on the old capitalistic economic doctrines of "laissez faire" is creating much more problematic situations than remedying the prevailing world problems that are discussed in the first three chapters of this book. In fact Chua (2003) posits that it is creating ethnic hatred and generating global instability.

It is critical to realize, once again, globalization, particularly the technology transfer aspect of it, can be the most important holistic solution to the problems of the fragile planet. But Darwinism let loose is more likely to exacerbate all of the problems rather than solve them. And, of course, if globalization is acting like Darwinism on steroids, the problems will emerge faster and in a much more intensified manner. Thus, equating globalization with laissez-faire capitalism that is accelerated, unchecked, and powerful will do more harm to the world's well-being. However, if capitalism extends its impact and adopts primarily the ambition factor, the resulting conditions and their outcomes can be very different.

How About Social Capitalism?

If the conditions within which capitalism functioned were to be made more equitable, then the benefits of the system could have, and should have, further reach to the whole society. This is what the author coins "social capitalism." In the simplest terms, it means not winner take all, but all participants to receive part of the benefits commensurate to their contributions. This would mean globalization benefiting everyone and taking full advantage of the four flows discussed earlier. This is not stopping or counteracting capitalism but modifying its laissez-faire version somewhat by, first, emphasizing the ambition factor and, second, using the basic premises of social capitalism as discussed here.

Social capitalism may be considered as a system in which many individuals or small companies develop collaboration. They provide each other with many different services and help. These partnerships may become larger alliances to tackle bigger projects. In such a model cooperation and a sense of community is likely to benefit the whole society. (Kaplan, Forste and Stahlman 2006).

Certain special features of social capitalism are presented in Exhibit 4.4 and discussed here briefly. If these features are intact, then most of the problems discussed in the first three chapters of this book can be remedied in a holistic manner. This will be the victory of modern capitalism.

Utilizing the Benefits of Technology

If, by applying science to economic problems, we could improve productivity, then the society as a whole should benefit. Thus, technological developments should not be simply replacing labor intensivity with capital and creating unused excesses

Exhibit 4.4 Essentials of social capitalism

Special feature	Impact	QOL implications
Utilizing the benefits of technology	Accelerated economic growth	Economic gains for the whole society
Infrastructure development	Increased productivity for all	Better QOL possibilities for all
Equal access to education	Better human resource management	Improved opportunities for better pay
Responsible environmental activity	Sustainable economic development	Steady improvement in QOL
Reasonable progressive income tax	Providing reasonable returns to labor's toil	Better participation in the economy's progress
Encouraging investments	Getting closer to full employment	Bringing the economy to higher plateaus
Better participation in the profitability of the firm	More limited ownership of the firm by labor	More income and greater motivation for all
Supporting entrepreneurial small businesses	More opportunities for talented and ambitious people	Further reach to the forgotten majority

in the society's labor supply. Technology, in terms of producing what could not have been produced before and doing this efficiently, by definition, must and, under proper circumstances, could benefit the whole society. This whole situation would accelerate economic growth and, to a significant extent, reduce the proportion of have-nots in the society. The situation prevailing in the third world is even more critical than situations existing in the industrialized world. In third world countries, in general, infrastructures are almost nonexistent. Because of this infrastructure deficiency, application of technological advances is likely to be less than adequate. It is critical that proper infrastructures will be developed so that the benefits of technological advances will materialize and be shared.

Infrastructure Development

Since infrastructure development is not a private sector undertaking, and since many capitalist governments feel a constant budget crunch, typically infrastructures deteriorate, which interferes with the economic progress of the society as a whole. Not only must the infrastructure be repaired and updated but it must also be improved scientifically. The more up to date the infrastructure, the greater the capability of the private sector to compete. Increased efficiency of technology due to advances made in the infrastructure, by definition, would improve the QOL prospects of all in the society.

Equal Access to Education

The most important resource of any society is humans. If, for some reason, certain sectors in the society do not have equal access to education, they will not be able to perform according to their full capacity. Again, such situations would lead to a widening between haves and have-nots.

Responsible Environmental Activity

All of Chapter 3 in this book is devoted to environmentalism or, rather, the lack thereof. A simplistic statement bears repeating: If the fragile planet does not survive, we cannot survive either. We must have technologies functioning in a totally non-offensive manner. Only under such circumstances will it be possible to develop sustainable economic activity. In addition to economic progress, responsible environmental activity would provide a better quality of life in terms of enhancing health and producing better-quality agricultural products. Environmentalism has been objected to by many on the basis of some costs they may incur in the short run. However, this is being rather shortsighted because of its impact on productivity, on health, and on the social psychology of the society; environmentalism is a valuable economic tool to enhance the overall quality of life in the society.

Reasonable Progressive Income Tax

Unlike the thinking of certain groups in society, income tax is not simply for the support of government, and government is not simply for the protection of the people against a military threat. Modern governments of the 21st century must play the role of socioeconomic and political leaders. As such, they are expected not only to stimulate the economic activity in the country but also to improve income distribution, education, health, and the quality of life (QOL). In other words, modern governments will have to play the role of a coach of a championship team. In order to perform such an important task, there needs to be a very serious revenue base. Here the authors believe that people will have to pay taxes commensurate with the benefit they receive from the economy. But it is critical that people with an annual income of millions pay more than, say, a mail carrier who makes very little money. Paying a fair share is substantially related to the benefits received from the economy. Thus, people must pay their fair share. The most important point here is that tax revenue should not be simply to take care of government's expenses but to invest in the society's educational health and infrastructure systems among other important activities. Such investments can yield greater return to the society than allowing individuals to spend their own money in any way they want through reduced tax rates.

Encouraging Investments

Investments by the private sector make profitability of this sector enhance if public investments are adequate. First and foremost, as discussed earlier, an adequate infrastructure is necessary. This is primarily a major public investment. A society without adequate energy resources, human resources, logistics resources, or communication facilities cannot possibly make adequate economic progress no matter how willing is its business class to invest. Investment opportunities must be present, and investments must be encouraged to create an almost, if not totally, full employment. Also, as mentioned earlier, a society's most important resource is its manpower. If and when everyone in a society is working, it means that all citizens are pulling their weight and participating in the economy's progress. Only reasonable investments would generate opportunities to absorb all of the citizenry of a society into productive and meaningful activity. This is, truly, how the country's economy reaches higher plateaus.

Better Participation in the Profitability

As it stands, 21st-century capitalism is enhancing the gap between haves and have-nots both domestically and internationally. Much of this is based on the greed factor that is encouraged by pure laissez-faire practices. Basing gains in the marketplace on the assumption of the presence of a zero-sum game, where somebody's gain is dependent on somebody else's loss, cannot possibly improve the already dismal economic picture of the world. As discussed earlier, this situation is serious enough to create class warfare within the country and international terrorism between countries. Thus, instead of *winner take all* for the capitalists, *everyone to participate* in the profitability of all of business activities is a better orientation in terms of fairness and an even better proposition in terms of motivation to work harder. First of all, the factors of production are not only capital but also land, labor, and capital. Thus, in terms of fairness, it must be understood that capital without labor cannot truly produce anything. It becomes meaningful for labor to participate in the profitability and the ownership of where the work is done. Perhaps one of the most important aspects of such ownership is not only its fairness, because of the widespread participation, but the motivation of labor to work harder, since the benefits accrue directly to the participants who are working harder. This type of stimulation will create a greater performance on the part of the economy and will seriously narrow the gap between haves and have-nots while both groups are making definite progress.

Supporting Entrepreneurial Small Businesses

Entrepreneurs are visionaries, starters, developers, and builders. They are typically small or medium-size businesses. As discussed in various sections of this book, not a top-down but a bottom-up globalization or a second wave of globalization is considered to be necessary to neutralize the negative effects of the current globalization process. This bottom-up or the second wave of globalization happens to be generated by entrepreneurial activity. Small entrepreneurs can do much in terms of reaching out to the forgotten majority of the world and satisfying the unanswered needs for handsome profits. This is a major activity in which global giants would not be engaged.

Globalization within the constraints of the ambition factor and social capitalism, as can be seen, can have an almost holistic approach to the problems cited in the first three chapters. However, the 21st-century capitalism must modernize its orientation from being driven by greed to driving for constructive ambition to advance and share the gains as much as possible. Thus the advancement in the direction of social capitalism is necessary if there is a future for the fragile planet. A brief introduction to this version of capitalism is presented in this chapter. It must be reiterated that the switch from winner take all to sharing the benefits according to contribution made is a major change in the current thinking. However, it is necessary to make such a change in the general orientation of economic and political thinking of this century. Without a viable social capitalism, the fragile planet is not likely to have a future. However, making such a switch successfully is hardly automatic. It will take a tremendous amount of thinking, planning, and implementing. The remainder of this book deals with the necessary specific steps to implement the holistic solution of social capitalism.

Summary

This chapter critically analyzes the pluses and minuses of globalization. Although globalization may be the only hope to cure major ills of the world, it is not functioning in that direction. The chapter presents few flows of globalization leading in the direction of acceleration of goods and services flow. Once again as pluses and minuses compared, the chapter indicates that globalization is running short in its benefits and is contributing to the increasing gap between the poor and the rich. But as globalization continues, some of the global companies are becoming bigger than nations and are ignoring rational and regional governments. They are not reaching out to poorer parts of the world. Furthermore, they are not generating enough jobs. Thus the chapter makes a case for social capitalism.

References

Chua, Amy (2003), *World On Fire*, New York: Doubleday.
Friedman, Thomas L. (2000), *The Lexus and the Olive Tree*, New York: Anchor Books.
Globalization (2001), London: The Economist.
Hertz, Noreena (2001), *The Silent Take Over*, New York: The Free Press.
Kaplan, Jeffrey, Forste, Eric Watt., Stahlman, Mark (2006), *Social Capitalism*, London: Hypermedia Research Center, Westminster University.
Samli, A. Coskun (1985), *Technology Transfer*, Westport, CT: Greenwood.
Samli, A. Coskun (2002), *In Search of an Equitable and Sustainable Globalization*, Westport, CT: Quorum Books.
Samli, A. Coskun (2004), *Entering and Succeeding in Emerging Countries*, Mason, OH: Thomson Southwestern.
Stiglitz, Joseph E. (2002), *Globalization and Its Discontents*, New York: W. W. Norton and Company.

Chapter 5
Generating Wealth in Societies

Our discussion, thus far, has revolved around the key problems of the fragile planet and changes in the ways the planet needs to be managed. If there is to be a future, sustainability of the planet is the ultimate prerequisite. It is suggested that globalization within the constraints of social capitalism can provide a holistic remedy. But, in order to implement this holistic remedy, it is necessary to understand how economic activity will generate wealth and how such a process can be made to function smoothly, both within the parameters of globalization and of national economies. In order to implement the holistic remedy of proper globalization with social capitalism underpinnings, it is critical that a particular orientation is adapted and maintained. This particular orientation is based on the process of generating wealth in societies. Although the details in carrying out certain functions may differ from country to country, the basic functional ordering of the wealth-generation process remains the same. Thus, the necessary orientation and commensurate basic functions must be carefully identified.

The Necessary Orientation

The general orientation for companies, regions, and countries has to be one of wealth creation and its equitable distribution. Here, like a jigsaw puzzle, all the parts must fit into a big picture. It is critical to realize that without such a picture in mind, the society cannot make progress. And if societies do not make progress, the fragile planet cannot survive. Exhibit 5.1 illustrates the key sequential order of such a wealth development orientation.

The whole process begins with creating and maintaining public order. Without such stability prevailing in the society, there cannot be any economic progress. Political and/or social unrest can definitely interfere with the economic progress of the society. In fact, even an advanced society such as Japan stopped its marvelous economic progress during the late 20th century as its political picture became unstable.

In order to maintain public order, as can be seen in Exhibit 5.1, it is necessary to have a power structure within and outside the country. A police force provides internal order, and an army maintains protection against outside agitation. Naturally

A.C. Samli, *Globalization from the Bottom Up*,
DOI: 10.1007/978-0-387-77098-7_5, © Springer Science+Business Media, LLC 2008

Exhibit 5.1 Creating wealth and distributing it

Source: Adapted and revised from Samli (2000).

both power structures are based on the guidelines identified by a legal structure which is totally essential for economic progress. The legal and power structures must provide the needed orientation for progress. Kotler et al. (1997) discuss the structures and the orientation existing in the four Asian tigers, which may be considered a very valuable and viable model. As was discussed earlier in Chapter 1, all four tigers of Asia had an active and fully participating elite which provided the necessary orientation for economic progress that can be described in terms of creating wealth and distributing it equitably. If the conditions of public order are met, then it is critical to redirect much of the attention to the infrastructure. In other words, reasonably powerful local governments with the support of economic power are the necessary ingredients of public order.

Developing the Infrastructure

Since economic progress in terms of wealth creation and distribution cannot happen without the infrastructure, this must be taken very seriously. Unfortunately, 19th-century capitalism did not pay much attention to this all-important concept.

But then, in their very simplistic model, the laissez-faire people did not even include government as one of the players (Stiglitz 2002). As has been pointed out earlier, governments are the key players in the development and maintenance of infrastructures since they do not, and indeed they should not, yield profit.

In 21st-century capitalism, without the infrastructure that provides energy, mobility, information, and basic facilities to produce, there cannot be major efficient mass producers in the society. Without mass production, it is difficult to assume the emergence or presence of economic progress. The infrastructure that is so necessary, but so unprofitable to develop efficiently by the private sector adequately, almost by definition becomes the government's purview.

Of course, in order to develop an effective labor force as well as a healthy and informed populace, it is essential that health care facilities and educational systems are properly advanced and functional. With the presence of public order and a friendly infrastructure, wealth creation-related economic activity is ready to commence. In this respect, generating new ideas and implementing them is critical.

Generating New Ideas and Implementing Them

Earthshaking new ideas such as developing a sequel to $E=MC^2$ may not be possible or even necessary, but practical ideas such as generating the most food value as cheaply as possible are necessary. For instance, sweet potatoes are rather easy to grow and have good food value, but are not known in many parts of the emerging countries. Some years ago, the biochemistry and nutrition department at Virginia Tech developed a concept named nutri-bun. The basic idea behind this product was to find the cheapest and most plentiful protein in a region and incorporate the protein into this nutritional product called nutri-bun. Developing, say, local facilities to produce such a product where a similar good does not exist would be an important new idea. Such a product will supply much-needed food value. It is critical that the society provide opportunities to individuals for new idea generation and implementation. As is discussed later on in this book, generation and implementation of new product or new process ideas are very appropriate for small and entrepreneurial businesses that have enough flexibility and foresight. It is not necessarily implied here that all emerging countries are or should be involved in primary research to uncover secrets of the universe, but the four flows of globalization, presented in Chapter 4, can easily generate new ideas that can effectively be put to use. These ideas may identify how prevalent these four flows and their offshoots are and how they can be adjusted to local conditions for optimal solutions. Needless to say, these new ideas, perhaps obtained through the four flows of globalization, can be carefully modified, adjusted, and used somewhat differently than the original thought or knowledge so that they can be used effectively for local needs and local conditions. It must be reiterated that local conditions can be a major deterrent of progress or a powerful enhancer of it. In order for people to generate and use new product and process ideas they must have the skills to not only take advantage of what might have been learned through, say, the Internet but also discover new knowledge. Holland used windmills for energy. Malaysia produces and exports rubber-based computer parts that are somewhat unique. It is quite possible that every country, every region, and even every company has possibilities to discover new knowledge, invent new products, and use them effectively in generating wealth.

Skills for Discoveries

It has been shown that a large proportion of private patents that are creating discoveries are based on knowledge generated by public sources such as universities, nonprofit organizations, and government laboratories. Without information generated by these organizations, there would not be a next generation of knowledge (Thurow 1999). Emerging countries are no exception. They can generate their own knowledge base. They also have a great advantage. All the information generated in the industrial world and in the organizations mentioned above is available. Thus, there is the possibility of using the available information in the world to the best advantage, rather than trying to reinvent the wheel. In fact, it has been stated that in the third world (or the emerging world), most countries that manage to make progress have done so by copying (Thurow 1999). Thus, many emerging country industrialists and scientists can take the available new information and adjust it to their needs and their country's needs. This way they actually have a head start in generating knowledge. Skills are needed not only for discoveries, but also to convert these discoveries into new products and processes and to use them.

As Thurow (1999, p. 131) stated: "In the 19th century capitalism, human skills weren't seen as that important. Labor was a rented, hired-and-fired, marginal factor of production." But today in the 21st century, it must be understood that human skills are the most critical starting point in the wealth creation activity. The 21st-century capitalism is being forced to put human skills and knowledge rather than machinery and capital at the core of the system.

Exhibit 5.2 presents the author's perception of education, skills, and creativity connections prevailing in key and identifiable parts of the world. As can be seen both in the United States and Europe, the top half and the bottom half of the society are different. In both places, the lower half needs more than what it has. In Japan, the upper and lower halves are quite similar, but perhaps the whole society needs a bit more creativity. In the third world all three – education, skills, and creativity – are lacking. It is maintained here that both skills and creativity require, first and foremost, a very sound educational base. With some effort, skills, at least partially, can be acquired on the job, but creativity requires serious educational effort. Exhibit 5.2 illustrates what is needed as a key starting point for the economic progress and concomitant wealth generation before the haves and have-nots will be able to bridge the gap between them as they all go to a higher level of wealth and quality of life. This whole activity is not a one-shot proposition. It will have to continue indefinitely. The benefits accrued from the activity must be further invested in industrialization.

Exhibit 5.2 Education and skill relationships

	United States	Europe	Japan	Third world
The top of the society	Well educated; highly creative with good skills	Well educated; moderately creative; moderate skills	Well educated; good skills; need more creativity	Need more education; need better skills; need more creativity
The bottom of the society	Need better education; need better creativity; has reasonable skills	Well educated; needs more creativity; needs more skills	Well educated; good skills; need more creativity	Need more education; need better skills; need more creativity

Investments into Manufacturing and Housing

As wealth accumulates, it is important that a major proportion of it be funneled into investment in manufacturing and housing. In 19th-century capitalism, making capital cheaper was good enough to generate investments. In fact, the remnants of this thinking still prevail. At the writing of this book, the political parties are debating about huge tax cuts that will go mostly to the richest members of society. The tax cuts and low interest rates are considered by Republicans as the sure formula for stimulating investments. This, in turn, would eliminate the prolonged recession that has been going on. However, above all, in the 21st century, the rich do not quite invest in businesses and start them from scratch. After all, they are quite comfortable and have no inclination to take unnecessary risks. They certainly prefer to play the stock market and participate in other financial activities such as mergers and acquisitions. The people who are likely to invest and take chances are the middle-income entrepreneurial group that has much ambition to get ahead. But even that group will not invest just because money is cheap. They will invest as market opportunities emerge. Such an ambitious entrepreneurial group, not only in advanced societies but particularly in developing countries, can be extremely useful in generating the desired economic advancement.

Some years ago Naisbitt (1982) referred to the changes in our society as moving from an industrial to an information society. However, no matter how critical and how advanced the information technologies, production industries and construction industries must be further advanced if our society is to achieve economic progress. This again is extremely critical for the emerging countries. They must be further industrialized and must generate economic wealth and consumer value. Here not only detecting opportunities but investing toward benefiting from them is part of the extremely critical characteristic of entrepreneurial classes in third world (or emerging) countries. Investment in manufacturing and housing implies the proper utilization of the society's manpower resources.

Housing, in this discussion, takes two distinct positions. First, better housing as claimed by many studies would enhance the productivity of labor, since better housing provides better rest and peace of mind. Second, better buildings for factories and other places of production would enhance overall productivity as well as would improve security. Investing in housing, or construction in general, must be taken very seriously in the process of wealth generation in a society.

The Society's Manpower Resources Must Be Utilized

At the time of writing this book, Europe had an over 10 percent unemployment rate. The United States, with those who have given up looking for jobs, has about 8 percent unemployment. But in most third world countries this figure is in excess of 20 percent or more. How the gap between haves and have-nots can be narrowed, under these circumstances, becomes a very critical question without a satisfactory answer. Instead of allowing terrorists to recruit angry and/or starving people to work for them, the West must find ways to stimulate the economies of third world countries, knowing full well that not only would this be an extremely effective counter-terrorism measure, but also, if their economies are developed, these countries will become better customers for Western products and services.

No other resource comes even close to the importance of human resources in a society. Unlike 18th- or 19th-century capitalism, 21st-century capitalism needs to put much more emphasis on this resource. Whereas in the 19th century, achieving full employment and hiring unskilled workers were commonplace, in the 21st century, skills and education are essential for the lower half or even lower two-thirds of the workforce, as it is in the top one-third of the workforce. In other words, opportunities for totally unskilled workers in the knowledge-based industrial economy are very scarce and are becoming scarcer in time. If and when there is a slowdown in the economy, much larger groups of lesser-skilled and educated workers find themselves out of work, and such developments in 21st-century capitalism must be taken into consideration. Negligence in these areas becomes too costly for the whole society because it interferes seriously with the process of wealth-generation process.

Instead of having a number of billionaires who have tremendous market wealth and concentrated economic power with which they control market conditions, characteristic of 21st-century capitalism at the writing of this book, a social capitalism is needed. Only if we rely more on the ambition factor and acknowledge that much of the value generated in the marketplace is based on the efforts of fully trained and competent labor to be placed can conditions in the fragile planet be improved substantially.

In other words, we must move away from a zero-sum society where the thinking is that one group gets richer only if the other group loses (in a sense a stagnant society). This is a society where everyone can win by generating wealth for all (a dynamic society) is the critical change that is needed for a modern 21st-century capitalism. Indeed, we presented the essentials of social capitalism in Chapter 4. Even though the 21st-century capitalism must move beyond its current status toward social capitalism, it is critical how the current status emerged. For instance, the critical role that is attributed to labor or the workforce in 21st-century capitalism does not compare to relatively less value attributed to labor in 19th-century capitalism. Labor in 19th-century capitalism was perceived to be a given. It was not considered nearly as important as it is in the 21st century. In some of the emerging countries where half of the population, the female gender, is ignored and not allowed to participate fully in the country's economic activity, there may not be an opportunity to narrow the economic gap between them and the advanced economies of the West. It must be reiterated that, first, the role of labor in generating wealth must be understood and, second, a female's role in the society must be enhanced. A country's human resources do not refer only to the male portion of the population. Females are equally important and must be allowed to get as much education as they can, build as many skills as they can, and, above all, they must be used in the economic activity of the society as fully as possible. Needless to say, females in the society must also receive remuneration commensurate with their toil.

Distributing Wealth Efficiently and Equitably

If a global market capitalism in its current form, which may also be called a free market democracy, were to be exercised, the generated wealth could hardly be distributed efficiently and equitably. Chua (2003) proposes at least four alternatives that may achieve a more equitable distribution of wealth and income: leveling the playing field, giving the poor a greater stake, promoting liberal democracies, and the dominant rich elite making the conditions more tolerable.

Leveling the Playing Field: This is, both within and between countries, making sure that the poor majorities have access to better (or some) education and better access to jobs. Educating the population as opportunities are created is simply the most important activity that might (indeed would) narrow the gap between haves and have-nots, regardless of whether the gap prevails within or between countries.

Giving the Poor a Greater Stake: Unchecked laissez fairism, by definition, leaves large numbers of the poor majorities totally behind without making an attempt to bring them the benefits of globalization. This is not only unacceptable in 21st century, but it is rather dangerous, since more and more people feel hopeless and helpless on the basis of excessive use of the greed factor. There may be different ways to help them participate in the benefits of economic growth through globalization. We may give direct remuneration, give them some property rights, give them an ownership stake, and, finally, implement affirmative action.

Promoting Liberal Democracies: In developing countries, if there is a semblance of democracy, it is nominal and not quite real. In such cases, it is critical that there be more than a simple majority rule. Here perhaps the Chinese approach of "markets first, democracy later" may be used. However, there is a serious question as to whether marketization can take place and work well without some semblance of democracy. But marketization may be the higher priority. If the marketization is very broad-based, it can work to everyone's satisfaction. But as Hertz (2001, p. 66) states, "Economics has become the new politics, and business is in the driving seat." Thus, in the 21st century, there is a very strong tendency (knowingly or unknowingly) to confuse capitalism and democracy. Both governments and businesses are redefining their positions to facilitate ever-increasing economic freedoms and market shares of the total economic activity, hence prioritizing the expansion of unchecked and unguided capitalism over democracy. In fact, by the same forces, there is serious propaganda maintaining that capitalism and democracy are one and the same. Such an orientation, by definition, is playing into the hands of the greed factor and contributing to the global economic inequalities in a geometric manner. The "geometric manner" term is used here to indicate an accelerating process in economic inequality, primarily, again, unchecked and unregulated top-down globalization.

Dominant Rich Elite's Role: If, in time, the extremely rich elite emerges and gains more and more market power and becomes more and more resented by the bottom of the pyramid as Prahalad articulates (2005), democratic opposites can be extremely destabilizing factors. In other words, giving political power without the economic power to the impoverished is likely to produce class warfare. Indeed, unchecked and uninterrupted, there may be real class warfare. Therefore, if there were to be global social capitalism in the current 21st century, its format primarily would be emerging in the form of volunteerism. This would mean, primarily, the voluntary actions of the powerful market-dominant minorities themselves (Chua 2003). Such social capitalism is most likely to eliminate the possibilities of class warfare. These market-dominant minorities can (and perhaps should) generate market opportunities based on their voluntary generosity. As they generate more opportunities in the marketplace, they can also lay down the foundation to generate multitudinous entrepreneurial opportunities. This self-motivated philanthropism in the short run may be the most workable way to develop and share wealth in poorer regions of developed countries and third world countries in general.

Generating and distributing wealth efficiently and equitably, without a doubt, is the most important solution to economic inequalities and cultural clashes. Our discussion thus far did not do much with the emerging militarism and environmental hostilities that are discussed in the first three chapters of this book. But as stated or at least implied in Chapter 2, improving the economic conditions, by definition, would eliminate part of the hostilities and with that happening, the emerging militarism will substantially subside.

In terms of the environment, as stated earlier, if the fragile planet does not survive, we cannot survive either. However, it may also be reiterated that positive environmental policies are likely to create jobs and help economic growth in the short run, and they are definitely an important stimulant of economic progress in the long run.

By understanding how wealth is generated in societies, it will be possible to implement specific remedies for the problems of the fragile planet. Once again, its problems must be understood and specifically coped with if we are to aim at building a better world. In order to really understand how wealth is created, we must critically analyze capitalism.

The Changing Parameters of Capitalism

Throughout Chapter 4 and the present chapter, our discussion revolved around 19th-century and 21st-century capitalism. If the differences between the two are not understood, and if the need for the changing nature of capitalism is not acknowledged, it will be impossible to cope with the problems raised in the first three chapters of the book. And if those problems are not resolved, then the fragile planet has no future.

Exhibit 5.3 illustrates some of the most critical discrepancies between 19th-century and 21st-century capitalism. As can be seen, perhaps more important than anything else, information has become more critical than money per se as the key source of power. After all, it is not money that created Microsoft or developed the personal computer. With the presence of critical knowledge in 21st-century capitalism, it is rather easy to find the necessary financial support. It is the availability and importance of information that generates monetary returns as a reward to the ownership of this power base.

In 21st-century capitalism, labor plays a very critical role. This is because the number of menial jobs is decreasing and typical labor-related jobs are becoming more and more demanding of skill. Those necessary skills enhance the core competency of the corporate entity and provide additional market power. As was mentioned earlier, in 19th-century capitalism, labor was primarily unskilled; therefore, any laborer could have been replaced by any other laborer any time. Thus, labor was treated like a commodity with very little value. The contribution of labor was not considered part of the wealth-generating activity.

Exhibit 5.3 19th-century capitalism versus 21st-century capitalism

	19th century	21st century
The source of power	Money was the total absolute power generating wealth	Information is the most critical force that leads to wealth formation
The role of labor	Commoditization of unskilled labor used as a given in wealth generation	Greatly needed skilled labor and its utilization for generating wealth
The value of human capital	Not needing skilled labor and not assuming that it generates wealth	The value of human capital is the pivotal activity in wealth creation
Intellectual capital	Did not exist and was not an issue	Extremely critical in corporate performance and wealth creation
The need for middle class	Was not an issue; there was always adequate aggregate demand	The need is very real since this group is important in generating aggregate demand
Environmentalism	Has never been an issue for classical capitalism since technology was simplistic and caveat emptor was the rule	A very critical issue since environmental issues interfere with profits of major players in the marketplace

Thus, the value of human capital is a new concept that is seriously attached to 21st-century capitalism. The company's labor force is its human capital that gives the company competitive advantage as it creates wealth and is rewarded by profits that it receives.

Being very simplistic in nature, the companies in the 19th century did not consider such a thing called intellectual capital. However, in the 21st century, the companies that innovate the most receive the first-mover advantage in the marketplace. The companies that have more patents are likely to use this intellectual capital to their advantage to make money. Thus, intellectual capital of the firm generates wealth.

In 19th-century capitalism, there were hardly any possibilities for executives to make multiple millions of dollars annually. Most businesses were small, and earnings were modest. Small businesses competed among themselves, and such competition created greater consumer value for large groups and helped generate a large middle class. Thus, having a large middle class was a natural outcome. But it did not necessarily mean much except in stabilizing the society. However, in the 21st century, the presence of a middle class is much more critical in creating and maintaining an aggregate demand that will keep the industrial production at a high level and generate wealth for the society. However, if Darwinism on steroids is allowed to take place at home and abroad, the future of the middle class becomes rather questionable. It is maintained that instead of expanding, the middle class is shrinking in the United States and everywhere else(Samli 2000).

Finally, in the 19th century, environmental problems were almost nil. Basically, the increasing complexity of life in general and some industries in particular has created a very serious problem of survival for the whole world. 21st-century capitalism finds itself up against the struggling fragile planet for survival.

Given these extremely significant differences between 19th-century and 21st-century capitalism and dramatically different social and economic conditions, it is very doubtful that 19th-century capitalism can help generate wealth in the 21st century. In fact, unless 21st-century capitalism requirements are met, the fragile planet cannot survive. It is extremely critical that how wealth is generated in a society is understood so that there will be more of it. Although the comparison between the 19th- and 21st-century capitalism indicates the greater capability of the 21st century to generate greater and faster wealth, this wealth and the economic power it represents are concentrated more and more in the hands of a few. Hence, the benefits of progress are not at all shared. With decreasing entrepreneurial competition, governments favoring big businesses, and nonenforcement of antimonopoly laws such as antitrust laws, 21st-century capitalism leaves much room for greed rather than ambition. The greater and faster generated wealth is substantially badly distributed among the populace, the more questionable is the whole system. It is ironic that 21st-century capitalism has a better chance to generate wealth but is strongly inclined to keep it in the hands of a few select people rather than the society as a whole. Thus, our discussions in Chapter 1 and in this chapter are not contradictory.

In both chapters, we are stating that the 19th-century capitalism stimulated more competition and hence encouraged ambition more than greed. The 21st century is much more capable of creating wealth and consumer value, but is encouraging more emphasis on greed than ambition. The author believes that ambition instilled in modern capitalism is good but does not go far enough. The 21st-century capitalism must take the form of social capitalism for the sake of the future of the fragile planet.

Summary

This chapter presents a very critical point at the beginning, sustainability. If the planet is sustainable there will be no future. The current capitalism combined with uncontrolled globalization is not providing enough impetus for sustainability. Instead, it is proposed that social capitalism could accomplish what is not accomplished as yet. A seven-step model is presented to enhance the sustainability of the planet from an economic perspective. These are creating and maintaining public order, developing infrastructures, new idea generation possibilities, investing accumulated wealth wisely, utilizing manpower resources fully, Facilitating breakthrough development, and distributing economic gains equitably. In order to accomplish such an agenda it is critical to go back to 19th-century capitalism which is depicted as ambition as opposed to 20th-century capitalism that is depicted as greed.

References

Chua, Amy (2003), *World on Fire*, New York: Doubleday.
Hertz, Noreena (2001), *The Silent Takeover*, New York: Free Press.
Kotler, Philip, Jatusripitak, Somkid, and Maesincee, Suwit (1997), *The Marketing of Nations*, New York: The Free press.
Naisbitt, John (1982), *Megatrends*, New York: Warner Books.
Prahalad, C.K. (2005), *The Fortune of at the Bottom of the Pyramid*, Upper Saddle River, NY: Pearson Education.
Samli, A. Coskun (2000), *Empowering the American Consumer*, Westport, CT: Quorum Books.
Stiglitz, Joseph E. (2002), *Globalization and Its Discontents*, New York: W. W. Norton and Company.
Thurow, Lester C. (1999), *Building Wealth*, New York: Harper Collins.

Chapter 6
Bottom-Up Globalization, Not Top-Down

Consider "O," a young Turkish entrepreneur-to-be. He borrowed a little money from a few relatives. He worked with his connections in the shoe-making cottage industry. He sold shoes to friends, to relatives, and also to other people as a street vendor. His business started picking up and he opened a store. The store was doing a reasonable amount of business. He decided to import some shoe-making machinery. After buying and assembling a number of such items, "O" started a small shoe-manufacturing operation. The factory started selling not only to the store that was owned by "O" but also to some other retailers in the region. On the basis of the performance of his retail shoe store, he decided to open other stores in different regions of the country. In the meantime, the factory expanded to cater to the needs of multiple stores. Through newly acquired acquaintances, he developed partnerships in Eastern Europe as well as Italy. Some 25 years later, almost 400 employees work in the factory, producing shoes for about 30 stores throughout Turkey that employ many locals and export to partnerships that "O" initiated in a number of countries. This is what is meant in this chapter by bottom-up globalization. It is not a global giant that entered the country to cater to the top tier market, not able to reach or not bothering to reach the bottom tiers and leaving majorities unattended. "O," on the other hand, started at the bottom of the pyramid in Prahalad's (2005) terminology and spread out. In doing so, he made a much greater contribution to the well-being of the forgotten majority than globalization in its current form.

When ministers of G-8 meet, one wonders if the advanced industrialized countries really understand the problems of what the author calls "the forgotten majority" (Samli 2004). In fact, because it is not G-200 (about that many nations are in existence at the writing of this book), one can easily conclude that G-8 governments are more concerned about themselves and their constituencies than the forgotten majority. In fact, it may be maintained that this is the continuation of 18th- and 19th-century imperialism. It is way overdue that a major conference of G-200 representatives be conducted. The G-8 governments still carry the remnants of historic imperialistic tendencies. Planning for and guiding of *underlings* by a central power has been the practice, at least during the past three centuries. Such practices in more recent times have allowed the emergence of super global giant firms that receive authority and power from multiple governments and practice a top-down globalization. Getting away from military might and concentrating on financial and

A.C. Samli, *Globalization from the Bottom Up*,   63
DOI: 10.1007/978-0-387-77098-7_6, © Springer Science+Business Media, LLC 2008

industrial might is a more modern form of centuries-old imperialism. When the International Monetary Fund (IMF) or the World Bank specifies the conditions of the loans that they make, and these specifications almost literally turn the receiving societies upside down (the Asian financial crises of 1999, Turkish crises of 2000, and Argentinean crises of 2001, among others), and when companies with budgets and economic powers greater than many nation-states make certain decisions and dictate the conditions under which they will conduct business in small countries or regions, they are exercising the modern version of imperialism. In today's globalization process, which is more powerful than individual local authorities, very powerful corporations and financial institutions are engaged in creating and managing the four flows that are discussed in Chapter 4. They do that selectively and with an authority that is directed from the top. Such a top-down orientation is evidenced by a meeting of G-8 rather than G-200.

The top-down globalization is exactly what Friedman (2000) stated: "Darwinism on steroids." One can easily argue that without such top-down globalization, there would be no globalization at all, but the top-down globalization without certain controls and motives other than profit cannot be sustained and hence, it is less than adequate (Samli 2002).

Although Hardt and Negri (2001) maintain that the modern globalization is the emergence of a new empire without boundaries and with more shared economic and financial power throughout the world, the realities of the world indicate that the wishful thinking by these gentlemen is not materializing and the empire (if there is such a thing in actuality) is achieving a greater divisionalism than economic progress for all. As Friedman (2000, p. 355) stated brilliantly "...globalization can create as many solutions and opportunities as it can problems." In its current format, globalization is creating more problems than solutions.

What Does Size Mean?

A third world country such as India has a market pyramid. This pyramid is composed of four tiers. The first tier is composed of seven million people with an income greater than $20,000. The second tier is represented by 63 million people who have an income between $10,000 and $20,000. The third tier involves about 125 million Indians making between $5,000 and $10,000. Finally, the fourth tier represents the rest of the society where over 700 million make less than $5,000 (Prahalad and Lieberthal 1998). Most developing countries have similar pyramids. The important point about the current wave of globalization is that global giants are likely to look at tier 1 and ignore the rest. However, tiers 2, 3, and 4 also represent clear-cut needs and a buying power that cannot be and should not be ignored. Subsequently Prahalad (2005) analyzed the same pyramid with five tiers. The bottom of the global economic pyramid is the fastest growth part of the world's population.

Pillsbury Doughboy on Indian television, it is reported, presses his palms together, bows in the traditional Indian greeting style, and speaks six languages. The Doughboy is promoting a group of higher margin products, such as microwavable pizza.

Pillsbury knows very well that it will appeal to tiers 1 or 2 in the Indian market. But there are almost 300 languages and over 800 million or more people that Pillsbury does not even attempt to reach. Thus a large majority is ignored. The same thing can be said for global giants such as IBM, Xerox, or Nokia. These firms would not appeal to tiers 3, 4, or 5 because these tiers represent small and less profitable markets. Instead, they would appeal to tier 1 and 2 of world markets, again ignoring and bypassing the majorities. The fact that these majorities are ignored is one of the major contributing factors to the problems discussed in Chapters 1 and 4.

By functioning primarily at the first two tiers and actively pursuing globalization, global giants exacerbate most of the problems that have been discussed in the first three chapters of this book. Simply stated, bipolarization of the world population, militarism, and environmental offensiveness are all the outcome of the current globalization process that the authors call top-down. Top-down means selective trickle-down of benefits to the upper tiers. Even though many global giants may not have ill intent in their normal trading activities, due to the lack of a global order and careful follow-up of the outcomes, the negative results become more intensified. The fact that global giants prefer to deal with the first tier, as discussed above, almost automatically creates and intensifies the negative impacts of their activities. Globalization carried out primarily by global giants, in the described manner, is not sustainable (Samli 2002).

The Problem with Global Giants

As Isaak (2005, p. 93) posits, "Globalization promises deregulation for the sake of prosperity – the privatization of everything possible. Hence, individuals can maximize their interests without limits to their freedom." Global corporate giants have been, are, and will be taking advantage of this orientation if nothing is done to reverse the situation. Perhaps the worst thing about this situation, as mentioned earlier, is that these giants deal only with the first two layers of the global economic pyramid. These companies are not quite equipped nor are they willing to cater to the lower layers of global economic pyramid;they have at least seven characteristics that may be considered handicaps that prevent them from reaching out and doing extensive business with these lower layers. They are far removed from remote, small, and scattered third world markets; they lack understanding of the prevailing needs in these markets; they have high operating costs and therefore they need critical masses that would buy their products in these markets; they are rather inflexible in making adjustments to sudden market changes that take place often in small third world markets; they lack speed in making corporate decisions because of the presence of multiple corporate layers; they are unable to implement the necessary marketing functions in remote, small, and scattered third world markets, and in general, the global giants are disinterested in emerging world markets since they are extremely gainfully occupied in the richest markets of the world. Thus, the current wave of globalization carried out by a number of global giants, by definition, is not likely to reach out and benefit the lower layers of global economic pyramid.

Thus, a second wave of globalization that is bottom-up rather than top-down is necessary to broaden the benefits of globalization and make it thoroughly sustainable (Samli 2004). In order to achieve sustainability and generate more solutions than problems, the current top-down globalization must be balanced with a bottom-up version of globalization.

The Needed Second Wave

Individually, smaller markets of tiers 3, 4, or, according to a recent book, 5 (Prahalad 2005) are extremely diversified, meaning that their tastes, their needs, their shopping habits, and their incomes all differ from each other significantly. Furthermore, these smaller markets are geographically scattered and difficult to reach. But combined together, they are bigger than combined tiers 1 and 2 (Samli 2004). On the other side of the coin, as stated earlier, global giants are too large to cater to the specific needs and whims of these very small niche markets. These giants are bound by the need to generate large-sale volumes and keep their market offering close to the "one-size-fits-all" approach. Their size, their expenses, and their specific needs to generate significant levels of income create certain degrees of inflexibility that typically prevent them reaching out to small markets scattered throughout the third world. But those markets also have serious needs and some buying power that cannot be ignored. They are much better target markets for local, small, and entrepreneurial enterprises. In the current world situation, these enterprises function alone and isolated enough that they do not benefit at all from globalization and its benefits perspective. In order for small businesses that are scattered throughout the third world to benefit from the globalization process and extend the benefits of this process deep into their own smaller markets and collectively to smaller markets of the world, they need to partner with small businesses from the industrialized countries. This is the key element of a bottom-up globalization that is proposed in this book.

Our discussion thus far does not imply that nobody is paying attention to tiers 3, 4, or 5, but only very few large firms would consider catering to these markets from the top. Prahalad (2005) makes a point that in tiers 3, 4, or 5, there is much money to be made, and some forward-looking companies are reaching out to these sectors and performing well. But this is only a small proportion of businesses, and many of the forgotten majorities are not being catered to from the top. Once again small, local, and entrepreneurial firms can reach these sectors easily and satisfy their needs more readily. This bottom-up orientation not only caters to tiers 3, 4, or 5 but also makes up for the harmful deficiencies of top-down globalization. It must be noted that the emergence of a bottom-up globalization has nothing to do with the current top-down globalization. It is assumed that they could easily coexist and jointly benefit the whole world.

Consider, for instance, two graduate students in business who started a small business of buying and reconditioning office equipment and selling it at very reasonable prices. Then they acquired a few partners in Latin America similarly exporting parts or components, reconditioning and selling them at very reasonable prices. The business is growing and helping other businesses that would not have the ownership of this equipment if they were to buy them new at their original market price. This is a typical example of reaching out to the forgotten majority in a bottom-up manner. There needs to be an upsurge of such activities throughout the emerging (or third) world. Developing such partnerships is not easy, so much special attention must be paid if the second wave of globalization is to be successful.

How Can We Get Lean, Mean Companies to Partner?

The second wave of globalization must begin with partnerships at the small business level where businesses are flexible, efficient, and more capable of catering to local needs and local whims (Samli 2004). As further discussed later on, they can create jobs much faster than their gigantic counterparts and, in general, are incomparably more creative in coping with problems that are extraneous to their beings. For instance, small businesses dominate Vietnam's private sector. They help the country's economy by partially alleviating the country's tremendous poverty. Encouraging entrepreneurship in that country is considered a major coup. Creation of a climate of entrepreneurship is needed everywhere in the third world.

Finding just the names of possible partners is critical. Although Exhibit 6.1lists seven specific sources of information about connecting with prospective partners, these specific sources, with the possible exception of international matchmakers, are not exclusively or even partially and deliberately in the business of connecting possible future partners.

It is critical to realize that any and all of the seven entities presented in Exhibit 6.1 can function as international matchmakers, but they certainly do not go out of their way to do so, with the exception of what is called here "international matchmakers." These entities, as seen in the exhibit, are a combination of private and public organizations. They are not widespread, but they are needed. Scandinavian countries are beginning to work in the direction of generating international matchmakers. These semipublic companies are exploring ways to bring small companies together to partner. This is what the present authors believe is the crux of the second wave of globalization that is going to be bottom-up and stop the imperialistic behavior of top-down globalization.

Exhibit 6.1 Sources of information for prospective partners

Agencies	Affiliations
• International Trade Organizations	Private
• National Embassies	Public
• Chambers of Commerce	Semiprivate
• International Matchmakers	Combination
• Ministries of Trade	Public
• National Industrial Directories	Private
• Direct Contact Through the Internet	Private

What Do Small Firms Have to Offer?

Samli (2004, p. 147) states the following: "A small company has almost no bureaucracy, no stockholders to report to, and fewer organizational layers through which information and decisions must seep." Small companies have specific characteristics that need to be understood and specific strengths that need to be appreciated. As a result of these special features, small firms can do certain things very successfully.

Exhibit 6.2 presents four key characteristics that small firms possess and which totally justify their being the focal point of the second wave of globalization. The characteristics of small businesses discussed here are applicable to both domestic and foreign small entrepreneurial entities.

Small Businesses Are Innovative

These businesses not only can generate new ideas, because of the lack of a large rigid corporate culture, but can also assess newly emerging opportunities in the marketplace. Because they do not have a rigid corporate culture, they can act on the ideas that are likely to be highly opportunistic.

Small Businesses Are Flexible

Being flexible means many different things. Many small businesses can detect if their strategic plan is not working well. In such cases, they can detect the problem early and change the strategic activity quickly and, if necessary, dramatically. If and

---

Exhibit 6.2 Special characteristics of small firms

- They are innovative
  - They can generate new practical ideas
  - They can assess new opportunities quickly
  - They do not have a rigid corporate culture
  - They can act on ideas quickly
- They are flexible
  - They can change the strategic activity quickly
  - They can adjust to sudden changes in the market
  - Planning and implementation of changes take little time
  - They can make major decisions very quickly
- They are very close to the market
  - They understand market conditions well
  - They are sensitive to consumer needs
  - They are familiar with consumer behavior
  - They can enter the market from lower end
- They are very prone to establishing partnerships
  - They can move faster in finding partners
  - They can become larger networks
  - They can work closely with network members
  - They can find trading blocks to be a member of

Source: Adapted and revised from Samli (2004).

when dramatic changes take place in their markets, small businesses can respond swiftly and adjust to these changes. Because of their organizational structures, small entrepreneurial businesses can plan and implement changes in their strategies quickly. Furthermore, they can make many important decisions very fast.

Small Businesses Are Very Close to the Market

These businesses, because of their close proximity, understand their markets well. One of their major advantages over their global and gigantic counterparts is that they are very sensitive to their customers' needs. This also means that they know their customers' behavior well. As a result of this market savvy, small businesses can enter the market from the lower end and penetrate the market.

Small Businesses Are Very Prone to Establishing Partnerships

Being devoid of rigid corporate cultures, small businesses can move very fast in finding partners. Again, because of such flexibility, they can work with these partners closely and become part of networks or even larger trading blocks. It is critical to realize that all these features are expected to be present in both domestic and foreign companies. But much of the time, small entrepreneurial businesses are so involved in what they are doing, they do not seek out foreign partners or engage in international activity of their own. They need the encouragement and guidance from one of the seven sources of information that are listed in Exhibit 6.1. It must be reiterated that the current globalization process does not supercede the global entrepreneurship that is described in this chapter. In other words, it is quite possible that the current wave of globalization can coexist easily with the proposed second wave. After all, these two are likely to function in different tiers of the existing markets. Part of the current globalization process is the capital flow. This flow is generated primarily by foreign direct investments. Foreign direct investments (FDIs) do not provide the same results as the proposed second wave would generate.

What FDIs Cannot Do

One flow of globalization as discussed in Chapter 4, capital flow or financial flow, has enabled FDIs to come into being and, because of this development, global giants such as Ford, General Electric, Nokia, and General Motors have been joint venturing, investing, and partnering. However, in all cases, they have been relying on the capital flow or FDIs in order not only to enhance their global presence but also to further establish a top-down globalization process which is referred to as corporate imperialism. Samli (2004, p. 170) states, "Despite its enormous benefits, globalization in its present form is failing. . .This is due to four main gaps, the lack of a world order, a trickle-down orientation, the ignoring of possible benefits to stakeholders and concentration on bigger markets of the world." Thus, the global giants, in their pursuit of profits from their global activities, are primarily relying on FDIs and concentrating primarily on the most promising international markets. But this top-down orientation is ignoring the major part of the world population. This situation is exacerbating the problems presented in the first three chapters. It is maintained here that this type of globalization cannot be sustained and the fragile planet is in trouble.

What FDIs cannot do, small partnerships can. As mentioned earlier, there is much money to be made in the third, fourth, and fifth tiers of third world markets, and in these markets, there are many unmet needs. While global giants may not be attracted to these markets or unable to function efficiently in such small, scattered, and varied markets, small partnerships can function in these markets quite well. The key here is that small entrepreneurial partnerships can easily enter the market from the lower end and satisfy these unmet needs. In the process, not only do they generate consumer value, but also they create jobs in local economies. This bottom-up orientation is a win-win situation in these neglected world markets. Their development is essential if the world has a future. However, perhaps the most important aspect of this development dwells upon developing successful partnerships so that the third world entrepreneur-to-be receives some capital, technology and know-how from its Western partner (Samli 2004).

Searching for the Right Partner

Exhibit 6.3 presents a seven-step process in searching for the right partner.

Step 1 – Original Contact

The sources of information regarding the availability and the characteristics of the prospective partners are identified in Exhibit 6.1. The Internet was not discussed earlier; however, it is perhaps the easiest and most practical way of generating names of prospective partners. Again, it is critical that someone initiates the search and the contact process. In the case of small entrepreneurial companies, an outside party, say, a chamber of commerce, may initiate the company's search for a prospective partner.

Step 2 – Communication

If and when there is a list constructed, a letter of intent needs to be sent to all candidates, since all of them may not have an e-mail facility. The original communication is critical for the follow-up. Thus the letter of intent may carry some broad but serious information.

Exhibit 6.3 Finding the right partner

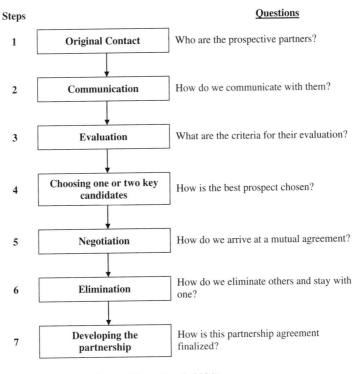

Steps		Questions
1	Original Contact	Who are the prospective partners?
2	Communication	How do we communicate with them?
3	Evaluation	What are the criteria for their evaluation?
4	Choosing one or two key candidates	How is the best prospect chosen?
5	Negotiation	How do we arrive at a mutual agreement?
6	Elimination	How do we eliminate others and stay with one?
7	Developing the partnership	How is this partnership agreement finalized?

Source: Adapted and revised from Samli (2004).

Step 3 – Evaluation

Since this is the first time and since the parties may not have had much experience in such an undertaking, evaluation is difficult but essential. Other books may provide more of the details of this activity (see for instance Samli 2004).

Step 4 – Choosing One or Two Key Candidates

It is critical to realize that one name and one contact may not work. Hence, one or two carefully selected additional candidates need to be identified and contacted. All of these candidates are likely to be good partners.

Step 5 – Negotiation

This may be the most important step in the whole process. The ideal situation is to have personal interaction leading to face-to-face negotiation. Here such activity can be very cultural. It is important to know the cultural taboos and not to make a mistake in this very sensitive process.

Step 6 – Elimination

In the final analysis, the parties will end up with one partner at one time or for the long haul. Here, previous steps of evaluation and negotiation will lead to the most important prospective partner. It is important to make sure that the best prospective partner is chosen.

Step 7 – Developing the Partnership

More essential than legalities or finances is that partners see eye-to-eye in establishing goals and plans for their implementation. Small entrepreneurial companies becoming partners is extremely critical, not only for the partners themselves but also for the second wave of globalization as well. This whole process, therefore, must be taken very seriously and must be supported as much as possible. One of the key advantages of the second wave is that regional and local developments precede globalization. This essentially means that local and regional political and cultural entities do not lose their identity. As was stated in Chapter 1, this is one of the most critical issues in the world's prevailing hostilities.

The Balance Between Foreign Influences and Local Control

As discussed in the first and fourth chapters, in its current form, globalization has created many companies whose budgets are greater than many national budgets of countries. Here there is a tendency for globalization and corporate entities to take over and ignore local or regional controls. Gaining more power than local governments makes these governments weaker and less able to undertake economic activity that would benefit their respective economies. Furthermore, such developments create serious hostility among the people residing in these regions. They react to the feeling that they are not important at all.

According to many, as globalization undermines local authorities, it is also putting pressure on local or regional cultural values. These values are questioned and, in some cases, rejected. As discussed in Chapter 3, these outside pressures are creating more clearly defined lines of demarcation and hostility on the part of the locals who are devastated by the "electronic herd" as Friedman (2000) coined the term. Thus, it is critical that, as the first wave of globalization continues with its scary vigor, the second wave of globalization somewhat balances it by empowering regional economies through bottom-up globalization implemented by small but effective partnerships. Local economic development and local controls are extremely essential to avoid deepening the lines of demarcation.

Partnering, the Necessary Ingredient

The authors believe that all the remarkable benefits of globalization can be achieved by third world have-nots if the second wave of globalization becomes a reality. It is proposed here that with partnering situations, there would be many problems that need to be overcome; however, if such a partnering orientation takes place, the benefits will offset the difficulties.

It must be reiterated that only such partnerships can reach out to the local people, generate consumer value, and also make a profit. Samli (2004) posits that such partnerships can expand into networks of many partners and eventually into trading blocks.

Bottom-up globalization is perhaps the only development that can nullify the dangers that the fragile planet is facing. But, such a development cannot emerge totally by itself. The industrial world must ignore some of the political pressures received from the global giants and must jointly support small entrepreneurial global partnerships. Certainly, the results of the second wave of globalization would prove to be much more beneficial for the world than simply allowing the current wave of globalization to continue to possible self-destruction.

Establishing the conditions under which the second wave of globalization will flourish is not easy. It will take certain specific activity to set it up and, more importantly, to develop a culture of entrepreneurship. These topics are discussed in Chapters 7 and 8.

Summary

This chapter takes a critical position about the current globalization which is top-down. It is maintained here that top-down globalization is crating a progressively worsening situation by widening the gap between the haves and have-nots. To balance some of the negative impact of top-down globalization, it is proposed to create and facilitate a bottom-up globalization. This entrepreneurial orientation can reach out to the forgotten majority in the world and cater to their needs effectively and profitably. This is because small entrepreneurial firms are innovative, flexible, very close to the market, and prone to develop partnerships. These partnerships can become networks and trading blocks. Thus, the bottom-up globalization can help narrow the gap between haves and have-nots.

Appendix: The Practice of Bottom-Up Entrepreneurships

Throughout this book, it is maintained that globalization based on the current thinking and practice of the primarily greed-driven 21st-century capitalism is top-down. In that sense, it is different from 18th-century capitalism which was driven by ambition. The current top-down globalization is not likely to stop and is not sustainable since the gap between have and have-nots is growing (Isaak 2005).

We are not suggesting stopping this top-down globalization for, at least, one reason that is in its current form, top-down globalization is unstoppable. It already has reached far too many corners of the world even through to the top of the global economic pyramid. In this book, we advocate that modern capitalism must pay more attention to a bottom-up globalization that will reach out to the bottom of the global economic pyramid which is primarily composed of the forgotten majority with much unsatisfied needs and limited means to pay for them. Global giants with technical and expensive products cannot reach them to sell their wares. Would these products be useful to the lower levels of the global economic pyramid? Can villagers in remote corners of the world who barely have electricity use these products? How can these people who live in poverty pay for these products? How would these products be promoted to the forgotten majority and how will they be distributed? These questions illustrate tremendous problems that global giants are facing and finding them insurmountable.

Thus, unless a bottom-up globalization activity is taking place the group at the bottom of the global economic pyramid will never get benefits of any globalization or economic advancement.

Throughout this book, we discussed indirectly the merits of a bottom-up globalization. In this appendix, the strategic thinking of the small entrepreneurial companies is presented. A local small company will have to consider at least six key components of a strategic action if they are to be involved in a bottom-up globalization activity. The six components of strategic action are product design, innovation, pricing, organizational development, competition, communication and distribution (Exhibit 6.4).

Product Design

Based on general characteristics and idiosyncrasies of the lower tiers of global economic pyramid, companies that are involved in bottom-up globalization must

Exhibit 6.4 The bottom-up strategic thinking

Small entrepreneurial companies' technical considerations	
Product design	Products must be simpler and more labor intensive
Innovation	Companies must innovate products and services to satisfy the peculiarities of emerging markets
Pricing	Products must be durable and extremely affordable
Organizational structures	Local simple networks to reach remote corners of emerging markets
Competition	By catering to local needs of the forgotten majority, locals can compete with global giants
Communication and distribution	By communicating with locals locally and reaching out to them through detailed distribution, small entrepreneurs succeed

Source: Adapted and revised from *Business Week*, September 27, 2004.

generate products that are smaller, simpler, and more labor intensive to produce than the products that are being traded by top-down globalization. Simputer, for instance, which is a durable handheld computer is developed and sold in India.

Innovation

Since all emerging markets have their own peculiarities and different varieties of needs, local companies must innovate products and services that are satisfactory for the peculiar needs of locals. In attempting to generate a product that would be simple to use and durable in harsh environments, for instance, India's TVS Electronics developed a new kind of all-in-one business machine which is part computer and part cash register (*Business Week*, September 27).

Pricing

The locally developed products not only must be durable but also must be very affordable. The TVS Electronics developed product, for instance, that costs only $180. In addition to simpler and less costly products, jointly used computers in kiosks and other innovations are making the prices affordable.

Organizational Structures

In order to reach out to the scattered and multiple local markets, where the forgotten majority resides, local simple networks are used. They know where the markets are and how to reach them.

Competition

Since local needs are different and local markets are spread out in multiple small sizes, local small entrepreneurial companies can more easily reach these markets and cater to their needs. This makes it possible for Linux, for instance, which is an emerging and powerful alternative to Microsoft, to function in some markets of China, Japan, and Korea.

Communication and Distribution

Communicating with the widely scattered emerging local markets calls for a better understanding of the characteristics and needs of these markets. Because of the lower literacy levels, brochures with detailed illustrations, packages and containers that are readily identifiable, because of the pictures and logos on them, are more useful. If there are certain local mass media, such as posters or signs in public transportation, they can be very effective (Samli 2004).

Finally, due to lack of transportation facilities, vast retailing operations needed to reach out physically to lower levels of the global economic pyramid. These markets are growing fast and local entrepreneurs are managing to reach out successfully and outdo the global giants. Communicating with locals locally and reaching out to them through spread out small-scale retailing appear to be quite effective in these markets. What is needed here is faster emerging entrepreneurial cultures.

References

Business Week (2004), "Tech's Future," September 27, 82–89.

Friedman, Thomas L. (2000), *The Lexus and the Olive Tree*, New York: Anchor Books.

Hardt, Michael and Negri, Antonio (2001), *Empire*, Cambridge, MA: Harvard University Press.

Isaak, Robert A. (2005), *The Globalization Gap*, Upper Saddle River, NJ: F T Prentice Hall.

Prahalad, C. K. (2005), *The Fortune at the Bottom of the Pyramid*, Upper Saddle River, NJ: Wharton School Publishing.

Prahalad, C. K. and Lieberthal, Kenneth (1998), "The End of Corporate Imperialism," *Harvard Business Review*, July–August, 68–80.

Samli, A. Coskun (2004), *Entering and Succeeding in Emerging Countries: Marketing to the Forgotten Majority*, Mason, OH: Thomson Learning/South-Western.

Samli, A. Coskun (2002), *In Search of An Equitable and Sustainable Globalization*, Westport, CT: Quorum Books.

Chapter 7
Double Entrepreneurship is Synergistic

- A textile company in Turkey teamed up with one in Brazil. Jointly they produce, sell, and export the inside layers needed for auto tires.
- A Swiss company brought into Turkey trucks full of fresh vegetables. The company partnered with a Turkish firm. At the present time, jointly they own hundreds of small grocery stores scattered throughout the region.

Being entrepreneurial and finding partners who are also entrepreneurial is the essence of bottom-up globalization. Countries, regions, and companies all must consider the benefits of such involvements.

The French economist Cantillon is said to have introduced the term "entrepreneur." He defined the term as the agent who purchased the means of production for transforming them into marketable products. The French economist J. B. Say expanded Cantillon's ideas around 1880. According to Say, an entrepreneur is a person who shifts economic resources out of an area which is not yielding good returns and does not have high productivity into an area that has higher productivity and greater yield; thus, the entrepreneur is the organizer of the business firm. Many years later Dewing (1914) viewed an entrepreneur as a promoter who transforms ideas into profitable businesses. According to Drucker (1985), the entrepreneur is the person who starts his own new business that usually is small. However, all new small businesses are not necessarily entrepreneurial. They must be creating something new and different to be called entrepreneurial. Finally, according to Schumpeter (1934), entrepreneurship is creative destruction where new entrepreneurship destroys the old and rather dysfunctional businesses and provides new and advanced versions. Schumpeter, who dealt with entrepreneurship early and in detail, posited that entrepreneurs bring about dynamic disequilibrium to the society, which he named creative destruction. But the authors believe that international entrepreneurship is not creative destruction; rather, it is creative construction.

An entrepreneur is a highly motivated and trained person who tries to perform well regardless of the nature of the job. He or she is an opportunity-seeker who looks for ways to improve performance. Simultaneously, the entrepreneur also tries to improve his or her economic status. The entrepreneur, therefore, is an achiever and creator who decides on the resources, skills, and capital that is needed and takes pride in high-level performance. The authors believe that what the international

A.C. Samli, *Globalization from the Bottom Up*,
DOI: 10.1007/978-0-387-77098-7_7, © Springer Science+Business Media, LLC 2008

entrepreneurs do is creative constructionism, which is of the highest importance for modern capitalism.

Particularly dealing with the third world, entrepreneurs are totally necessary to improve economic conditions and, hopefully, narrow the gap between the haves and have-nots by reaching out and satisfying the needs of the forgotten majority, while making a profit.

In Chapter 1, the author has made an important reference to the "greed factor." Nineteenth-century capitalism was different than 21st-century capitalism in the sense that even though the greed factor was, has been, and is always present, and indeed in the 19th century there were some who practiced and got away with their greed factors like robber barons, the conditions were such that there were more entrepreneurs motivated by ambition rather than greed. Additionally, the governments were much more friendly toward small businesses and the enhancement of competition. Thus, in the 19th century, conditions were more suitable to exercise ambition than greed. Hence, capitalism made a much more significant impact in terms of improving economic conditions than the capitalism of the 21st century. In this century, there is less competition due to an endless merger mania, and the laws that would enhance competition, such as antitrust laws, are not enforced properly and adequately. Entrepreneurship, by definition, indicates the presence of more competition that would encourage the ambition factor but would go against greed. Even if there were no international partnerships of entrepreneurs, just generating an environment suitable for the emergence of any local or regional entrepreneurial groups is extremely desirable.

Conditions Conducive for Entrepreneurship

Exhibit 7.1 illustrates three separate forces that will generate entrepreneurs.

These are macroatmosphere, personality characteristics, and external unexpected events.

Exhibit 7.1 Conditions conducive to entrepreneurial development

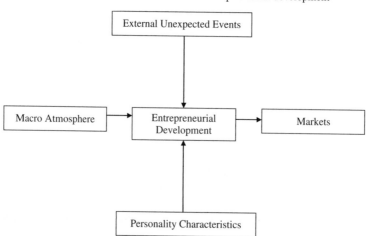

Macroatmosphere

The macroatmosphere or macrodimensions that are conducive to nurturing an entrepreneurial culture include at least four extremely critical factors. These are cultural characteristics, attitude toward small business, government support, and availability of information.

Cultural Characteristics

As indicated by Hofstede (1983), different cultures have different risk-perception and risk-aversion orientations. He discussed this broad factor in terms of uncertainty avoidance (Hofstede 1983). As Samli (1995) stated, in some societies people are trained to accept things as they are, and they live day to day without worrying about future uncertainties. They take risk rather easily, without exaggerating the possible negative consequences. In such cultures, it is more likely that there will be a more widespread entrepreneurial spirit. Similarly, some cultures are more open; they learn from other cultures not only how to develop businesses but also how to run them. Once again, those cultures may have a more widespread entrepreneurial spirit. Finally, one of the cultural traits that stimulate entrepreneurship is the trust factor. In some cultures, particularly in those that are identified as high-context cultures, interpersonal relationships and trust among people are rather common (Samli 1995). In such cultures, it will be easier to stimulate the entrepreneurial spirit.

Attitude Toward Small Business

Since entrepreneurial activity is primarily related to small business, a country's attitude toward small business is critical. Some cultures pay more attention to large business giants, often as a result of donations given by these firms to political parties. In such cases it is rather difficult to foresee a desirable expansion of entrepreneurship. By the same token, other cultures particularly encourage small businesses. Under such encouragement, it is reasonable to expect a thriving entrepreneurial activity.

Government Support

Somewhat related to the discussion above, it is not only the culture but the government that may be leaning in the direction of supporting small businesses and providing entrepreneurship with numerous support benefits such as tax advantages, research grants, and other direct and indirect help. In some of the emerging countries, governments have started business ventures, such as banking, manufacturing, or farming, and sold them to the private sector. Without such a variety of help and entrepreneurial orientation, entrepreneurship in many emerging countries cannot flourish.

Availability of Information

Private or public sources must have information regarding local, regional, and national economies, business conditions, and critical economic changes so that business opportunities for entrepreneurs can be identified. Presence of such information is not a natural activity. Therefore, special effort must be directed into generating such information. Here, there is a special need for the public and private sectors' cooperation so that best possible information can be made available for the entrepreneurs-to-be. Information about entrepreneurial opportunities must be evaluated, prioritized, planned, and carefully made available to the entrepreneurial talent in the society.

It must be reiterated that unfortunately there are hardly any attempts to construct the proper macroenvironment for entrepreneurship. The third world countries do not fully appreciate their need for entrepreneurship, and developed countries do not go out of their way to develop more and better knowledge of entrepreneurship that can be transplanted to the third world. However, it is clear that unless the macroconditions are in place and facilitating entrepreneurial efforts, nothing is likely to happen. It is also important to realize that a set of personality characteristics be present that are required of an entrepreneur. Everyone cannot be an entrepreneur, but all societies have entrepreneurial talent that needs to be cultivated.

Personality Characteristics

There are at least five personality characteristics that an entrepreneur-to-be must possess. These are vision, proactivity, interpersonal skills, friendliness, and problem-solving ability.

Vision

What makes an entrepreneur, above all other characteristics, is vision. If Thomas Edison did not have the vision of capturing sounds on tape, the recording industry would not have been born. If Sony's founder had not thought of entertaining those bored runners, there would not have been the Walkman. The entrepreneur-to-be must be in a position to study economic conditions at the local, national, and international levels, identify business opportunities, prioritize these opportunities, and initiate a business accordingly.

Grameen is a bank established in 1983 in Bangladesh and has concentrated on providing the poorest Bangladeshi people with miniscule loans. It supports personal initiative, helps the recipients to start minor enterprises thus recipients become self-sufficient and contributing members of the society. Since its establishment Grameen Bank has loaned out $3.8 billion to 2.4 million families in rural Bangladesh (Yunus 2003).

Consider a tropical flowers business, which was originated in Brazil. First it was operating only in domestic markets. However, considering possibilities in international markets it connected with local cooperative to produce its flowers and entered some European Markets successfully.

Beginning in 1976 a young eye doctor opened a private 11-bed clinic in India with a mission of eliminating needless blindness which existed extensively in India at the time. Many years later today that private clinic serves the poorest people in rural India and its one of the largest eye care system providers in the world.

A company with the name INFOSYS founded in India in 1981 started out with numerous IT projects such as testing, documentation, and the like, worked its way to coding then to designing, and subsequently to managing the entire IT systems. The company passed $1 billion revenue mark in 2004.

An American entrepreneur with the name of Gary Goldberg decided that he may combat allergen-related illnesses. He started a company with the name of Clean Brands. The company has developed a unique line of mattresses and pillow covers named Clean Rest Products that prevent sleepers from inhaling allergens such as dust mites. Clean Brands is succeeding in the United States and extending into South Korea, China, and some Latin-American markets. There are endless examples of similar success stories depicting the possibilities of bottom-up globalization.

Proactivity

Closely related to vision, the entrepreneur or an entrepreneur-to-be is an action-oriented person. Once the business opportunity is identified and selected, the entrepreneur does not waste time in becoming active in that proposed business. The entrepreneur's proactivity lies in the ability to start a venture that is not conventional and quite likely at the cutting edge of the practice, swiftly and without hesitation.

Two graduate students in the United States from Chile, after receiving their MBAs, have decided to sell reconditioned office equipment purchased in the United States, reconditioned and sold in Chile. Being able to see an opening in the market is critical for proactivity.

Interpersonal Skills

An entrepreneur is not a dictatorial manager who orders subordinates to perform certain tasks without allowing them to ask questions. Rather, an entrepreneur works with others as partners, coworkers, and people who are needed to accomplish jointly shared goals that will make the proposed undertaking successful. The entrepreneur is what Drucker (1985) calls the modern manager who does not work with a group of subordinates but with a group of partners. Thus, the entrepreneur possesses interpersonal skills to motivate and direct a group of people to perform optimally as coworkers or as partners.

Friendliness

The success in the interpersonal skill utilization comes from the entrepreneur's friendly disposition. He or she genuinely believes in what is being done and how it can be accomplished by working very closely with a group of friends who are also coworkers. Of course, that friendship feature also spills over into external relationships with suppliers and with prospective customers as well as actual customers. In some ways it almost appears as though relationship marketing concept, which emphasizes doing business by establishing long-lasting relationships, has been developed for entrepreneurs, for they work with an incessant enthusiasm and friendly disposition toward all parties that are involved in the particular project (or business). Knowing the customers' names, what they like, and how they behave are parts of the friendliness factor.

Problem-Solving Skills

As an entrepreneur undertakes a business venture, there will be many small and big problems that need to be resolved. Most of these are related to the performance and survival of the business venture that is just commencing. In all cases the entrepreneur's ability to make decisions and to solve problems is extremely critical.

Without being involved in a discussion regarding whether these personal characteristics are innate or learned, it can be reiterated that without their presence, the objectives of entrepreneurship cannot be fulfilled. There is one additional key dimension of the thriving entrepreneurial culture, coined by Drucker (1985) as "external events."

External Events

As seen in Exhibit 7.1, there is a third key dimension to entrepreneurial activity. There are numerous external events which could be included in this concept. An entrepreneur observes both slow and immediate changes in the marketplace and makes profitable adjustments in the business to take advantage of the opportunities that are opening up. Four such events that may stimulate entrepreneurship unexpectedly are discussed in this section. These are economic conditions, health-related events, a high-tech breakthrough, and changes in lifestyles.

Economic Conditions

Sudden changes in economic conditions may stimulate certain dynamic small businesses to become more entrepreneurial and find quick and effective solutions to their own dilemmas. Developing low-cost high-efficiency products in a recessionary period has been practiced by many small American firms.

Health-Related Events

These may take different forms and different directions. For instance, the suddenly increased popularization of holistic medicine may bring about retail outlets offering many products and services closer to consumers. Similarly, an increasing special interest in healthy living may generate entrepreneurial gyms and other exercise places for the population. Recently low-carb foods and menus have become very popular in the United States. Companies and restaurants can take advantage of such a development, and indeed, many have.

High-Tech Breakthroughs

Development of electric cars, for instance, could bring about special service places primarily for such cars. A development in software systems can stimulate many entrepreneurial activities to come into being. An IT system geared for small enterprises can be extremely useful for the enterprises and profitable for the developer.

Changes in Lifestyles

These changes can bring about many entrepreneurial small businesses. If, for instance, the society becomes more casual, many small apparel manufacturers can generate new products and distribute them in an entrepreneurial manner, say, through kiosks. Similarly, increased leisure time activities may bring about new and different entrepreneurial coffee houses.

These are only a few examples of what can be considered endless lines of opportunities.

Thus, small and dynamic entrepreneurial businesses are flexible and efficient. They can reach out deeper into wider dimensions of the market than gigantic corporate entities.

An Entrepreneurial Culture

Obviously, not just a few successful entrepreneurial undertakings, but an entrepreneurial culture needs to be developed. Such a culture would generate practical new products and services as well as more jobs. Thus, domestically an entrepreneurial culture is highly desirable, and for third world countries, a necessity.

Creativity Must Be Stimulated

If third world economies are likely to develop to a point of bridging the gap between them and their developed counterparts, creativity must be stimulated. This is not necessarily the creativity that would invent, say, the AIDS vaccine, but creativity toward using local resources, cutting corners, and manualizing capital-intensive production facilities, since third world countries have much more labor than capital. Almost by definition, creativity goes hand in hand with entrepreneurship. If a culture of entrepreneurship is constructed, again by definition, there is respectable room in that society for creativity. The points of the macroatmosphere are discussed in Exhibit 7.1. In this diagram, governmental support and availability of information are particularly critical if innovation and creativity are to be encouraged. Here government can easily make the tax burden very palatable for small businesses, while making education in small business management very powerful and available. Similarly, start-up funding, such as that which the U.S. Department of Commerce's Small Business Institute provides, is not only advisable but necessary.

Availability of information, as mentioned earlier, is also critical for creativity; for these authors believe that without adequate information, there cannot be much creativity, particularly if that creativity is dependent on business conditions and gaps in the market, among other critical items.

Leadership Characteristics Must Be Cultivated

Entrepreneurs are leaders in their own capacity within a set of reasonable proportions. They are not like generals or national heroes, even though they could be. They exercise leadership characteristics by being visionary, bringing a group of good people together, creating an atmosphere for optimum productivity, and running a business successfully. Without resorting to a highly theoretical issue of whether leadership is "innate" or "learned," it is possible to stimulate vision by making the entrepreneur's job easier and by providing educational endeavors such as short courses, seminars, and the like. The point here is that there must be a concerted effort to create and cultivate leadership as part of the expected economic progress. According to the present author's experiences, such activities are extremely few and far between, partially because the third world countries are involved in a struggle for survival on a daily basis and do not have the resources or the vision for the specifics of stimulating creativity, building leadership, and the like.

Performance Must Be Supported

Although what has been said in this chapter regarding creativity, leadership, and entrepreneurship are all applicable to the performance, there are other considerations as well. First and foremost, successful entrepreneurship activity must be identified, rewarded, and passed on to other entrepreneurial aspirants. However, such activities may intimidate some of the industrial giants and go against the greed factor we discussed in the first chapter. There should not be any possibility for the industrial giants to stifle the performance of entrepreneurs. This includes the industrial giants buying out the successful entrepreneurial ventures. This does not mean that conditions should be adverse to large businesses that mean well and work hard;

it simply means that size should not be a pure advantage in terms of power, and that large corporations cannot push smaller entrepreneurs around.

From Market-Dominant Minorities to an Entrepreneurial Culture

As was discussed earlier in Chapters 1–3, the four Asian tigers, i.e., Singapore, Taiwan, Hong Kong, and South Korea, are blessed with the presence of a very active intellectual elite who are hands-on participants of the economic progress. These are called by Chua (2003) as market-dominant minorities. Perhaps the most significant challenge is to move from market-dominant minorities to an entrepreneurial culture that will have enough self-starting power to improve the economy as the minorities make money. This is perhaps the most important aspect of market economies. If the markets are functioning well, then the profitability of the business sector is connected to the consumer value such a sector generates. This proportionately is not an automatic happening without any checks and balances being present. All the features of an entrepreneurial culture must be examined, and programs must be developed to cultivate the necessary entrepreneurial culture. Each third world country may have its own approach, its own priorities, and its own preferences, but the necessary effort to create a culture of entrepreneurship must be prevalent and functional.

Entrepreneurial Alliance Management

Having an entrepreneurial culture in the society is necessary for the economy, but it is truly synergistic when entrepreneurial cultures of different countries function together. In other words, entrepreneurs of Country A start partnering with the entrepreneurs of Country B. Thus, both countries start benefiting from internationalization and double entrepreneurial relationships. Such an arrangement, as illustrated in Exhibit 7.2, can generate at least two types of synergy, relational synergy and performance synergy. While the relational synergy deals with bringing the two parties to function in unison, performance synergy would create optimality in the joint performance of the partners.

Relational Synergy

In general, the lack of relational synergy would mean inadequate commitment by the partners. In order to avoid such a situation, there must be adequate sharing of information so that both parties are informed about, say, the market conditions, key economic development issues, and the like. The information-sharing activity must lead in the direction of communication so that the parties are properly in touch. Needless to say, both parties must be trustworthy and feel secure with each other.

Exhibit 7.2 Partners' expectations in double entrepreneurship

Synergistic Patterns	Expected Outcomes
Relational Synergy	The Partnership Functioning in Unison
Information sharing	Both parties are informed
Communication	Information flows in both directions
Security	Both parties are trustworthy
Control	Parties have equal control
Planning	Planning performed jointly
Performance Synergy	Partners Displaying Optimal Performance
Flexibility	The process can be modified once and adjusted
Productivity	Joint productivity is greater than individuals
Promotion	The joint organization is better promoted
Distribution	Neither party can succeed alone

Source: Adapted and revised from Samli (2004).

One party cannot have more controlling power than the other one. It is critical that both parties control the total process jointly. Finally, the plans for the future of the partnership must be constructed jointly to both parties' satisfaction.

Performance Synergy

Clearly if the partnership is likely to make progress, the performance synergy must be at its best. The partners, individually as well as jointly, must be flexible enough so that they can respond to unexpected changes and unusual demands in the marketplace. Needless to say, if the third world economies are going to make a move forward, the proposed partnerships must display high levels of productivity. When partners join forces, the productivity level goes up. Since partners are from different countries, the joint promotional activity must be more powerful than the individual efforts of the partners prior to the partnership's emergence. Finally, jointly, partners would complement each other so that they could achieve more than they could have achieved otherwise.

More Emphasis on Endogenous Growth is Needed

Perhaps one of the most critical problems prevailing at the dawn of the 21st century is that poor nations do not know how to develop their economies and are expecting help from industrialized countries. As is implied throughout this book somehow this proper and adequate help from outside is not coming. Less-developed countries end up owing much money and going in the wrong direction. Thus these countries instead of relying on exogenous economic growth must concentrate on endogenous economic growth (Bharadwaj, Clark and Kulviwat 2005). All countries have resources and potential for economic growth but putting these all together into a meaningful combination is not easy. The proposed bottom-up globalization discussed in this chapter is a partial answer. To complement the bottom-up globalization which starts with entrepreneurship a Silicon Valley facsimile is proposed.

Exhibit 7.3 Steps in developing a Silicon Valley facsimile

1. Develop an ecosystem that will attract and stimulate learning and innovation
2. Create an intellectual center to bring smartest students to facilitate local growth
3. Support entrepreneurial culture that generates new ways to accelerate and use innovations
4. Strategically locate these facilities to be close to academe as well as industries
5. Generate internal financial support for cutting-edge research that is suitable for endogenous growth
6. Build industrial parks mushrooming around the core of the Silicon Valley facsimile
7. Help support the development of a stable political economic system that would not be politicized
8. Enhance the sensitivity to cutting edge ideas leading to unique applications
9. Encourage networking, commitment and trust among and within teams
10. Manage the development architecture and infrastructure of a model community

Source: Adopted and revised from Isaak (2005).

Such organization can facilitate endogenous economic development and help the poor country to improve its economic status.

Exhibit 7.3 presents a ten-point process to develop a Silicon Valley facsimile. It is called facsimile here because it will never be exactly the same as the American version of that organizational complex. Each country's Silicon Valley has to take the form that is most suitable for that particular country.

Exhibit 7.3 steps are self-explanatory; however, it must be emphasized that the facsimile above all must stimulate learning and innovation to the extent that the best minds in that country are gathered there. The Silicon Valley facsimile supports an entrepreneurial culture that will create most suitable innovations for that country. Such innovations are based on the cutting-edge research that is undertaken by the facsimile. Needless to say such an undertaking demands the support of local, regional, and national governments. A stable and nonpolitical economic system is a necessary condition for such an undertaking. Politicizing it creates discontinuity and dramatic changes in its direction that would be dysfunctional. Acculturation of scientific and technological advances that are taking place around the world to the emerging country's needs can be achieved primarily by a well-functioning Silicon Valley facsimile.

The entrepreneurial alliance management, according to the present author, must follow at least three key principles. First, international entrepreneurial alliances should not and could not afford to undermine local needs. As was mentioned earlier in Chapter 1, a major problem with globalization as it stands is that local, regional, or national authorities are ignored. Weakening of local authorities creates much insecurity among the masses. Second, international alliance management must take manualization and utilization of labor extremely seriously, since for some third world countries, people resource is the only resource they have. Third, the present author believes that entrepreneurs can more readily and easily use the unused people power in these countries than global giants. Finally, a powerful entrepreneurship culture must be fully supported by a Silicon Valley facsimile which is to adopt global knowledge advancements to the culture and needs of the emerging country.

Summary

This chapter proposes utilization of entrepreneurship for bottom-up globalization. It is posited here that unlike Schumpeter's orientation (1934), entrepreneurship is not creative destructionism but creative constructionism. It is further maintained here that when entrepreneurs start partnering with other entrepreneurs the outcome is synergistic. In addition to discussing the personality characteristics of entrepreneurs, the chapter presents some external events that stimulate or necessitate emergence of entrepreneurship. Generating an entrepreneurial culture and stimulating creativity entrepreneurial alliances must be managed. This situation calls for endogenous economic growth. Endogenous economic growth will be facilitated by what is coined in this book *Silicon Valley Facsimiles*. The chapter presents a ten-step development of such an institution. Furthermore the chapter proposes that each developing country needs a Silicon Valley facsimile which is geared to the country's specific needs.

References

Bharadwaj, Sundar, Clark, Terry, and Kulviwat, Songpol (2005), "Marketing, Market Growth, and Endogenous Growth Theory: An Inquiry Into the Causes of Market Growth," *Journal of the Academy of Marketing Science*, Summer, 347–359.

Chua, Amy (2003), *World On Fire*, New York: Doubleday.

Dewing, Arthur Stone (1914), *The Financial Policy of Companies*, New York: Ronald Press.

Drucker, Peter (1985), *Innovation and Entrepreneurship*, New York: Harper and Row.

Hofstede, Geert (1983), "The Cultural Relativity of Organizational Practices and Theories," *Journal of International Business Studies*, Fall, 75–89.

Isaak, Robert A (2005), *The Globalization Gap*, Upper Saddle River, NJ: Prentice Hall.

Samli, A. Coskun (2004), *Entering and Succeeding in Emerging Countries*, Mason, OH: Thomson, South-Western.

Samli, A. Coskun (1995), *International Consumer Behavior*, Westport, CT: Quorum Books.

Schumpeter, Joseph (1934), *The Theory of Economic Development*, Cambridge: Harvard University Press.

Yunus, Muhammad (2003), *Banker to the Poor*, New York: Public Affairs.

Chapter 8
Toward Additional Key Solutions

If the fragile planet has a future, that future will come primarily from leveling the playing field. In Chapters 6 and 7, we discussed that the leveling of the playing field is very much dependent on creation of entrepreneurial cultures in third world countries. Entrepreneurs, unlike their industrial giant counterparts, can reach out to the forgotten majority (Samli 2004) because they are closer to consumers, more sensitive to consumer needs, more flexible and more responsive to market changes. But above all, emphasizing the development of an entrepreneurial culture would help to nullify the ill effects of the greed factor by replacing it with the ambition factor.

In Chapter 7, the specific conditions for the development of an entrepreneurial culture are spelled out. But a culture of entrepreneurship requires the presence of numerous conditions that are costly. It is advocated in that chapter that these conditions are not primarily by endogenous development programs. Additionally, the problem of being economically very poor and making progress very slowly, if at all, requires attack from all directions. Hence, exogenous economic development efforts must not be totally ignored. On the contrary, when possible, both endogenous and exogenous economic development efforts must coexist. In this chapter, we discuss some of these attack strategies that will improve the economies of the emerging world countries, hence minimizing international terrorism and domestic class warfare. The fragile planet's future depends on it. It must be reiterated that emphasizing these solutions does not preclude the boost that entrepreneurial activity requires to flourish.

Rebuilding Infrastructure

Building or rebuilding the existing or nonexisting infrastructure is so essential that it is difficult to comprehend why it is so often ignored in many third world countries. But it is ignored, for numerous reasons. First, infrastructure development is not quite visible and has no political appeal. Thus, instead of working with the information system or energy flow, a leader in the third world can gain much support by building an automobile factory which is visible and macho.

A.C. Samli, *Globalization from the Bottom Up*,
DOI: 10.1007/978-0-387-77098-7_8, © Springer Science+Business Media, LLC 2008

Second, infrastructure development is ignored because of the lack of knowledge. Unfortunately, it is still rather common that the role of infrastructure in a nation's economic productivity is not understood. In the third world (or the emerging countries), almost no national budget allocates major sums for the development of the infrastructure. Even if there were attempts in this area, with the lack of experience and the lack of knowledge as to how to proceed, progress is seriously deterred.

Third, the lack of resources is particularly important. The private sector does not enter into infrastructure development, since it is not profitable. Governments often believe they have more imminent problems to tackle. Typically, after some of the perceived problems are considered in a national budget, there will be virtually no funds left for infrastructure development. It is not conceivable to make serious economic progress with less than adequate transportation facilities, inadequate information flow, not enough energy supply, and other key considerations that account for infrastructure. It is extremely critical that improving the level of the playing field for the third world be made top priority if there is hope for the fragile planet.

Eliminating Causes of Terrorism

Terrorism may be somewhat new to American society, but has been going on for decades in many third world countries. It truly does not contribute much to the general well-being of countries and regions, but surely makes the future of the fragile planet even more questionable. Part of the domestic terrorism can be traced to the greed factor we have presented in Chapters 1–3. Many local warlord types, for some historical reason, play into the emotions of other local people, hoping that secession from the federal government may take place and they may become the leaders. Such developments cause much drain in the limited budgets of local and national governments that are trying to maintain peace. Certainly, there may be justification for complaints stemming from ill-treatment and discrimination; however, armed encounters make the situation much worse. Perhaps the most critical issue in such cases is that without peaceful conditions, economic progress cannot take place. Thus domestic terrorism and similarly serious class warfare are dangerous for a culture of entrepreneurship to emerge and progress. The industrialized world must find peaceful solutions to such dysfunctional and draining events. Perhaps an extension of the United Nations or the development of world courts may provide some answers.

More, Better, and Fairer World Trade

As discussed in Chapter 4, top-down globalization is here to stay. It is benefiting a few but not improving the quality of life of the forgotten majority. There is no doubt that more and more trade will take place and will lead to more expanded globalization. This process is very powerful and, if its negative impact can be neutralized, it can be a very good thing. It is critical that top-down globalization be matched or even excelled by bottom-up globalization.

Perhaps the worst aspect of the ever-expanding world trade is that a questionable greed principle prevails, that is, *the winners take all* (Friedman 2000). Whether the winner is a global giant or a local industrial powerhouse, winning for them is a good thing. Just how much of the winnings seep through the social hierarchy and reach the masses is a critical question. As has been discussed in Chapters 1–3, here a top-down industrial imperialism is at work. This top-down power display provides a very nominal trickle-down type of benefit to all participants, whose number is quite limited, which further creates ill will among those who do not receive any benefit and even lose their jobs because of advanced capitalization or automation of the production procedures.

Both domestically and internationally, participants in trade must receive some equitable remuneration that would make it worthwhile for them to work harder and produce more. Proportionality of the distribution of gains as opposed to "winners take all" is a must. It is proposed in this book that a bottom-up rather than a top-down globalization along with domestic industrialization would enhance the suitability of an entrepreneurial culture.

In order to achieve the objectives stressed in this section, there will have to be better negotiation that will not allow one party to take advantage of another. International courts to hear grievances need to be organized. Domestically, countries must have fairer progressive income taxes along with better minimum and even possibly maximum wages. These have to be accomplished without stifling initiative and, at the same time, not allowing the greed factor to raise its ugly head.

Ever since international economics and international trade theories have been formed, terms of trade have been an issue. Unfortunately, such a topic is not even discussed in current discourses. However, determining how the terms of trade need to be established and how each and every participant receives a favorable return must be given a higher priority in enhancing greater and fairer world trade.

More Beneficial Technology Transfer

Perhaps the most critical aspect of modern globalization is the technology transfer. Whereas the countries of the third world do not have the required resources to develop extremely sophisticated technologies, they are very capable of utilizing already developed and transferred technologies. In fact, in many instances, these technologies are adapted to local needs for better results. Indeed, what gave the Asian four tigers their start in becoming newly industrialized countries (NICs) happens to be the technologies transferred from the developed countries. For years, the South Korean firms Samsung and Emerson produced products for Japan. In order to make this happen, the Japanese gave the technology that they developed to the Korean companies. Needless to say, South Korea has many educated and entrepreneurial business leaders and a highly educated labor force; however, without the head start the country received through this technology transfer from Japan, nothing could have happened in terms of South Korea's becoming a newly industri-alized country.

The emerging world countries individually or jointly do not have the resources to start a major industry such as an automotive or computer industry; however, they have small and flexible entrepreneurial enterprises that are capable of adapting the technology and adjusting it to local needs and local resources. Again, such capabilities lend themselves to international entrepreneurial partnering. These part-nerships, unlike the global industrial giants, are flexible, sensitive to local market needs, able to reach out to remote corners of markets, familiar with the markets, and cost efficient. They can function in the varied and scattered markets of the third world. They can innovate modest changes in products, and they can generate new jobs. Thus, their contribution to the economic development of the region or nation is very substantial. Exhibit 8.1 presents a summary of the importance of such entrepreneurial alliances.

Although throughout this book we touched upon these topics, the six features of entrepreneurial alliance presented in Exhibit 8.1 need more careful discussion. These points are extremely critical in the 21st-century capitalism. Once again, healthy markets generate healthy profits. The specific features displayed in Exhibit 8.1 are critical in the overall health of global markets. If used properly, these features will certainly improve the size and quality of the emerging world markets. It must be reiterated that entrepreneurial companies dealing with, say, the fourth and fifth tiers of one economy can partner with similar companies in other countries and develop alliances.

Flexibility

Emerging world markets are spread out, more varied and more vulnerable to sudden changes than existing world markets. Here international entrepreneurial alliances, being close and more understanding of these markets and their changing needs, can respond quickly and effectively.

Exhibit 8.1 Advantages of entrepreneurial alliance

Feature	Benefit
Flexibility	Can make changes quickly to adjust local markets
Localization	Having a local touch makes the partnership more acceptable
Ability to outreach	Satisfying the needs of forgotten majority
Requiring limited funding	Ability to operate economically
Familiarity	Ability to operate effectively as against idiosyncrasies of remote and scattered markets
Innovativeness	Ability to adjust the product to local needs, manualize, and invent modified products for local needs

Localization

Particularly in emerging countries, being local for a company means that the market identifies itself with this firm. This situation makes the alliance more acceptable by the local market, since the company is aware of local conditions and in touch with local consumers.

Ability to Outreach

Small local entrepreneurial alliances can reach out to fringes of markets that would be impossible for global giants to reach out to. This would be not only physically difficult for them but also not profitable. The entrepreneurial alliances, hence, have a greater ability to outreach successfully and profitably.

Requiring Limited Funding

Most small entrepreneurial alliances, unlike their gigantic global counterparts, function with much less funding. They are typically more economical and efficient and less demanding of capital outlays.

Familiarity

Being rather local in nature and familiar with the conditions that are influencing their markets, entrepreneurial alliances are familiar enough to satisfy the idiosyncrasies of scattered and small markets. They can operate effectively and cater to varying local needs.

Innovativeness

Small firms, almost by definition, are in better position to innovate ways and means to satisfy local needs better than their global gigantic counterparts. They can develop or modify products and services rather easily to cater to unique needs and requirements of local markets.

Involving the Poor and Underprivileged in Economic Activity

It is critical to realize that the labor intensity that prevails in third world countries can be an asset as well as a liability. Unused human resources in the presence of high unemployment rates could be a major burden on an economy. This scenario is very common in third world countries and certainly a very critical deterrent to economic progress. Involving the unemployed, who most likely are poor and underprivileged in the industrial activity, is by far the most important solution to economic backwardness. Here manualization that is discussed earlier can be considered a major step in that direction. Almost by definition, we may be dealing with a labor-oriented capitalism. If that excess labor cannot be absorbed and put to use for productive endeavors, it will be nearly impossible for a country or a region to make major economic progress. Much of the time, an excess labor force is composed of the poor and underprivileged. But this unused source of human resources must be put to work if the expected manualization of the technology is to occur. There may be many other ways of absorbing the poor and underprivileged into mainstream economic activity.

Better Distribution of Economic Gains

Perhaps the worst aspect of the 19th-century capitalism, which is even more exacerbated in the 21st century, is the fact that the winner takes all. Even though the winner was driven by ambition in the 19th century, power and wealth became concentrated. In the 21st century, capitalism accelerated the greed-driven imperialism which domestically and internationally colonized certain groups that did not have the economic power to protect themselves and forced their existence into mainstream of economic activity. Indeed, the winner perhaps deserves to have a larger share of the earnings but the winners truly did not get where they are totally on their own. They had much help from other on the way up. One must consider that without labor, there can be no capital. It is therefore of the utmost importance that all the people who were part of that winning process are paid according to their contribution to the final winning picture. Here, not only must there be more favorable distribution of payments to all participants but with the global giants' help and encouragement, local governments must develop fiscal policies that will make the economic playing fields fairer for all participants. Partially the economic gains must find their way into the medical care and education of the poor and underprivileged, knowing full well that these segments of the population are one of the keys to economic progress. One may say that such economic progressiveness is essential to bridge the gap between the haves and have-nots throughout the world. As discussed in Chapters 1–3, such improvements invariably would reduce the prevailing hostilities and reduce the incentives to participate in terrorism or be engaged in class warfare. This is truly going to the root cause of terrorism, rather than spending billions of dollars toward counterterrorism activities that are not proved to be necessary or effective.

Social Capitalism Once Again

In Chapter 4, the concept of social capitalism is discussed. Once again, if it were possible that the activating powers of capitalism and making its accrued gains more available to the masses, meaning that not only a select few but all can receive not equal but proportional benefits to their efforts, then globalization, both top-down and bottom-up, can be extremely beneficial. As discussed in Chapter 4, this form of capitalism can bring about optimal benefits from the utilization of technology, from infrastructure development, from greater access to education, from environmental responsibilities, from progressive income taxes, and everyone takes some of the profits. Social capitalism may bridge the gap between democracy and the free market dichotomy. It may show its power through dynamic entrepreneurial cultures supported by Silicon Valley facsimiles.

Slowing Down Procreation

One topic that is so essential to the future of the fragile planet is population explosion. Just as any restaurant or hotel that is approved by the fire department has a seating or occupancy capacity, the fragile planet also has a limit to support so many people. Thus, irresponsible and endless procreation is almost a death warrant for the fragile planet. Clearly, the rate of procreation is much greater in the third world than the industrialized countries. Partially, if not fully, the reason for this is the insecurity of the population in the third world. Much of the time families have many children as insurance for their old age, since there are no retirement programs, no social security, no Medicare and the like. Controlling population explosion in these countries is closely related to generating programs that would eliminate insecurity about the future. Reiterating a very important point, the world cannot have a bright future if third world countries are in a race as to which one can procreate faster. Clearly much family planning information, along with a promised secure future, can reverse the current picture that appears to be irreversible.

More Compassion is Necessary

It is not compassionate conservatism but compassionate progressiveness that is needed throughout the world before the fragile planet goes too far into oblivion. Compassion does not really mean just being good or doing good selectively to some others, but creating equal opportunity in terms of education, health care, economic advancement, and so forth. The key concept here is not equality which cannot be reasonably achieved, but equal opportunity. It is critical that all members of societies throughout the world have an equal opportunity to be as good and as productive as they can be. As discussed throughout this book, if people consider they are giving up their own well-being for others' advancement, in other words, if they are perceiving the economy as a zero sum game, the greed factor sets in. Similarly, those who already have tremendous economic powers who are already suffering from the presence of the greed factor are in a position to continue squeezing out economic well-being from the poor and underprivileged, resulting in a rather remote chance for the fragile planet to make major economic progress. There must be a creative and progressive income tax and fiscal policies throughout the world to reverse this seemingly hopeless situation.

Once again, it is clear that enhancing equal opportunity for all, slowing down the rate of procreation, and converting the greed factor into an ambition factor are obvious solutions. The question arises as to how do we proceed in unison toward accomplishing these solutions. Perhaps at this point we go back to Chapters 1–3 of this book and take the position of not militarism, not suspicion, not lines of demarcation, but understanding that the fragile planet, if it is to have a future, its different factions must not quite be divided but, indeed, must be united.

The four Asian tigers, i.e., Singapore, Taiwan, Hong Kong, and South Korea, have shown that progress, however less than perfect, can be made (Kotler, Jatusripitak and Macencee 1977) and such progress, as a first step, needs to be carried much further. As one of the present authors posited, it is not the meeting of representatives from G-7 countries but a meeting of the representatives of the G-200 that must take place and be repeated on a yearly basis (Samli 2002). Not a divided, but a united world can possibly save the fragile planet.

Summary

This chapter proposes that endogenous and exogenous economic development efforts must coexist. Here, rebuilding infrastructure, eliminating causes of terrorism, generating more, better, and fairer world trade, and generating better technology transfer are the key areas that need to be considered. However, the main activity is still entrepreneurial alliance which is the necessary key solution for the world's economic doldrums. Such alliances have flexibility, local character, ability to outreach, not requiring excessive funds, familiarity with local markets and innovativeness.

References

Friedman, Thomas (2000), *Lexus and the Olive Tree*, New York: Anchor Books.
Kotler, Philip, Jatusripitak, Somkid, and Macencee, Suvit (1997), *The Marketing of Nations*, New York: The Free Press.
Samli, A. Coskun (2002), *In Search of an Equitable Sustainable Globalization*, Westport, CT: Quorum Books.
Samli, A. Coskun (2004), *Entering and Succeeding in Emerging Countries*, Mason, Ohio: Thomson, South Western.

Chapter 9
If They Win, We Win

Throughout this book, we tried to reiterate the idea that ambition is a good motivator and it is within the constraints of social capitalism. Similarly, we have argued that the greed factor is an extremely negative force, since it is based on the understanding that the world economy is a zero-sum game and economic gains can come only from others' losses. This force is also embedded in capitalism. Thus, left alone, capitalism could go in either direction. While one is very constructive, the other is totally destructive. We also posited that in the 21st century there are more opportunities and greater tendencies to go in the direction of the greed factor. Top-down globalization unchecked and unregulated, without a bottom-up globalization to balance, governments' particular interests in helping the global industrial gigantic enterprises and choosing capitalism over democracies, allowing economic powers to accumulate indefinitely in the hands of few are all responsible for this situation. It has also been asserted that with the greed factor in full swing, the fragile planet does not have much of a future.

The World Economy Is Not a Zero-Sum Game

Some 40 years ago, a Nobel prize-winning Swedish economist wrote a major book that was titled *The Asian Drama*. The author articulated how Asia and Asians are doomed with no hope for Asian economies to recuperate. The hopelessness described by Gunnar Myrdal (1968) was extremely discouraging. However, today as we look at many parts of Asia, including the four tigers, the People's Republic of China, and even India, it can be stated that there is significant progress. As this progress took place, the West, including the North American continent, Western Europe, and Northern Europe, also made significant progress. In other words it is not that one country made significant economic progress at the expense of another. This is a rather simple proof that the world economy is not based on a zero-sum game meaning that a country cannot make economic progress unless another country loses. Thus, there is much room for the ambition factor rather than the greed factor. If one were to construct a setting for a social capitalism which would be sharing the benefits of capitalism with the whole society, it would be critical to make sure that it is based on the ambition branch of capitalism rather than the greed branch.

A.C. Samli, *Globalization from the Bottom Up*,
DOI: 10.1007/978-0-387-77098-7_9, © Springer Science+Business Media, LLC 2008

World Markets Must Develop

It is clear that the fragile planet cannot make any progress unless world markets are developed. This is a necessary condition for the world's future; however, there are many other provisos along with the development factor. First, a discussion of the development aspect and then some comments on the other requirements are provided.

Perhaps the most important aspect of the development of world markets is related to expanding employment. Human resources are the most important resource of any country. They must all be absorbed, employed, and utilized in some way toward the development of the country.

Expanding employment, by definition, enhances buying power and hence satisfies the most unsatisfied needs of the consumers. Better housing, better nutrition, better education, among many other aspects of consumers' lifestyles, are likely to further create more demand and enhance the prevailing quality of life.

Additionally, the remote, scattered, and small third world markets must be given major consideration for the satisfaction of their basic needs through entrepreneurship.

As the markets of third world develop, their existing scattered and unreachable portions are likely to be brought into the mainstream, such developments would reduce discontent, unhappiness, and resultant tendencies to be part of international terrorism and eliminates possibilities of domestic class warfare. Entrepreneurship here becomes a real shield against such possible catastrophes.

Not only economic growth but also the distribution of this growth must be considered. If the third world markets were to grow and become better places for more business and improved quality of living, the economic growth must be measured more on per capita than national totals. National totals do not show fairness or lack thereof as per capita figures indicating fairness in distribution would indicate. If the fragile planet has any future, there must not be many people left behind as economic progress is taking place. The economic growth must be connected not only to present conditions but also to future potential. Building future growth potential is a necessary component of the much-needed economic progress.

It is critical to understand that many consumer needs and desires are going unanswered at the present time. As the world markets, particularly third world markets, develop they become better customers of Western products and services. Increased free and fair trade, by definition, is not only beneficial for all parties involved but is also critical to bring parties together. The more that trade takes place between parties, the more are communication, understanding, and closeness among them. The author maintains that peace through trade is much more achievable than peace through arms and military might. But if the world markets were to be further developed much more effort is needed to generate more new jobs. Small entrepreneurial businesses are known to be more successful in this endeavor than their gigantic global counterparts.

From Winner Take All to Proportionality

In attempting to improve the distribution of income, everywhere, accounting systems and tax systems can make some progress. Going back to an earlier statement, it is not equality but equal opportunity that needs to be practiced. What is meant by proportionality here is that no one runs an extremely successful business alone; it takes many people to make a business successful within an organization and many other organizations that are connected with the winning company. They all have contributed to the total profit picture; however, they are likely to receive some remuneration that is much less than the role they played in the final profit picture until some fair proportionality that would treat all contributors according to their contribution to the total picture. Thus the winner does not take all, and all others who are attached to the activity in question are motivated and compensated according to their efforts. Without such orientation, both domestically and internationally, capitalism is functioning on the basis of the greed factor rather than the ambition factor. Once again, without the ambition factor, international capitalism is not likely to help the future of the fragile planet. Proportionality in distributing the revenues or profits is essential in bringing the ambition factor into full force to play a most important role in improving the world's economic problems.

Getting Ready for a War Is Not It

As we have seen in Chapter 2, much money is spent on military preparedness, and there seems to be no letting up in sight. In fact, as the lines of demarcation are more and more established and powerfully identified, there is almost no alternative but to accelerate the efforts of military preparedness. This whole situation exacerbates the powers of the greed factor. More and more sophisticated military hardware is produced by some global oligopolists who control the main portion of the market and are not likely to encourage the reduction in the existing and/or accelerating international tensions.

If war or military preparedness is slowly but surely replaced by peace preparedness, there will be tremendous amounts of financial resources released for the economic and cultural solutions of the problems that exist in the fragile planet.

In marketing discipline, there is a statement which posits that it is five times more costly to get new customers than to make existing customers satisfied so that they will stay with a business. It is quite obvious that it will be much cheaper to maintain good relationships with the world than to create lines of demarcation and expand the military powers to points of no return. Such display of power is not only costly but also very dangerous. In the efforts of accumulating military hardware, it is quite possible to have miscommunications and accidental encounters that may threaten the sheer existence of the fragile planet.

As we have observed from the Iraq war, military preparedness does a very good job in winning the war, but not a very good job in winning the peace. Without winning the peace there is no future.

Instead of war preparedness, a better world to live in would result from peace preparedness, by better communication, by globalization, by international entrepreneurial partnering, and by emphasizing diplomacy rather than arrogance. Connecting themselves to the opportunity factor rather than the greed factor, parties will have enough resources to remedy the situation of desperate poverty and unbelievable gap between the haves and the have-nots.

No Tanks, Just Tractors

As early as the 1950s, America started giving "foreign aid" to some countries. However, much of the time this particular aid went directly to the prevailing power structure in these countries in the form of military aid. If those in the existing power structure were totally disliked by the masses, nothing happened in terms of a needed change, since those in power got stronger with the military aid. This situation explains the very complicated and ill-conceived Vietnamese war which was extremely counterproductive, both for that part of the world and the United States.

It is not clear that the lesson is properly learned, as since the Vietnamese war, the United States has gotten involved in two Iraqi wars. The second Iraqi war is a total nightmare, since winning the peace was not at all planned. The lesson first and foremost is establishing communication with those who may be considered adversaries or potential adversaries, and then providing tractors or key technologies, but not guns, to certain parties. This basic orientation must be prevalent in all parties so that quick and effective progress takes place before it is too late.

There Is Still Hope

We are trying to reiterate that conceivably it is not too late yet; however, every passing day is creating more and deepening problems for the fragile planet. Here, once again, there must be a G-200 (or the most recent count of independent countries) summit to make sure that the whole world is on the same wavelength and communications are progressing to all parties' satisfaction. It is clear that much is needed from the world community if we want to change the economic course of the world. Here no nation must be accused of terrorism or being called an axis of evil, knowing full well that these are subjective value judgments and they need not be used in a loosely and indiscriminant manner.

It is clear that if we expect the world community to change its orientation and develop a more friendly and more understanding outlook, there must be, above all, open, frank, and factual communication. Without such open communication, there will always be some doubt and some suspicion blocking the emergence of good will.

The presence of open and extensive communication could lead in the direction of better understanding and elimination of lines of demarcation. This means elimination of hostilities. If hostilities can be eliminated, then the general orientation can be changed from "guns to butter," meaning that the fragile planet is receiving the attention it needs and deserves.

Make War on Global Poverty

As opposed to a war-like stance on the part of the parties on their side of the lines of demarcation and noncommunication, if all parties declared war on world poverty and lack of education leading to lack of understanding, the world could clearly make significant progress.

It must be posited here that the position taken throughout this book is not just wishful thinking. The present authors believe that the world's problems require worldwide solutions. Global poverty cannot be eliminated with a few altruistic projects. Particularly from the perspective of the ambition factor, it is obvious that progress in any part of the world will spill over to other parts, unlike the greed factor that assumes progress in one part of the world will come about from a loss in another part of the world. In other words, if they win everybody wins, or if we win, everybody wins as well.

Yes, Virginia There Is a Future

The world is not going in the wrong direction per se, but its inhabitants are. It is clear that much more attention needs to be paid to the total global implications of the individual actions. During the cold war era, the presence of a *domino theory* was acknowledged. According to this theory, if a country goes communistic it will influence other neighboring countries to go communistic as well. Is it not possible to revive the domino theory in an opposite direction and say if certain countries are going in the direction of economic recuperation, their neighboring countries also can be part of this new domino theory and go economically, militarily, and culturally positive?

Yes, Virginia, there is or there may be a future for the fragile planet, but its inhabitants must understand that they no longer live in jungles where survival is due to being the enemy. Rather, united, there could be much progress and a great promise for the future.

The Win-Win Scenario

Exhibit 9.1 illustrates a win-win scenario. That scenario, in a sense, is the essence of this book. Elimination of hostilities and lines of demarcation based on a positive and effective global communication process, by definition, will minimize the need

Exhibit 9.1 The win-win scenario

for military preparedness. Elimination of hostilities, combined with minimizing the greed factor and maximizing the ambition factor, brings about the win-win orientation. Critically one may label this whole process as replacing hard *military power* with *soft communication power*. For instance, at the writing of this book, America is experiencing a very low overall image because of the Iraqi war which is not popular among many nations of the world. Thus, America's overall image has been tarnished. Instead of asserting more military power (hard power), it is possible to be engaged in more constructive worldwide communication with all nations and assert once again America's fairness and understanding of world problems, reversing the dangerous patterns of threat to the fragile planet. This kind of soft power utilization is not only much more effective and much more promising, but also much less expensive and dangerous. The bottom part of Exhibit 9.1 is critical. Throughout this book we not only covered the ambition factor, but also put some emphasis on the role of existing governments. The leadership provided by the government combined with the active and constructive intelligentsia mentioned in Chapter 5 makes it possible for the local economy to respond somewhat positively to the threat of globalization. The leadership in Singapore used exactly this powerful combination of powerful governments and a rich elite. Yew (2000) describes the role that government played in developing the remarkable Singapore economy. An eight-point model is presented in Exhibit 9.2. It is clear that the government paid much attention to helping the private sector flourish as the local and national resources are utilized effectively.

Exhibit 9.2 The role of government

- Attracting foreign investments
- Developing the infrastructure
- Helping the development of well-planned industrial estates
- Equity participation in industries
- Fiscal incentives and export promotion
- Establishing good labor relations
- Constructing sound macroeconomic policies
- Paying attention to the fundamentals that enable private enterprise to operate successfully.

Source: Adapted and revised from Yew (2000).

It must be understood thata a proactive central government is a critical variable in generating a win-win scenario but this author believes that a *power troika* is basically needed to do the job just right. As is discussed in Chapter 12 the power troika is the proper composition of the current top-down globalization, the hands-on government, and the entrepreneurial bottom-up globalization. All three together can accomplish much. Exhibit 9.2 illustrates the specific steps that the Singaporean economy took. In some ways the country benefited from a facsimile of power troika, the results of the efforts of the private and public sectors. Singapore today is one of the most thriving economies.

Summary

The chapter makes a critical assertion that the world or its future is not a zero-sum game. In other words, in order for the world to make economic progress, some bodies must lose out. This is the critical stance of the greed factor. Instead, the world markets must develop not only by generating more economic output, but by making it distributed more equitably. This will call for modification of the winner-takes-all principle into everyone receives benefits proportionate to the input one individually puts into the generation of the additional economic wellness. Countries must learn to communicate softly rather than muscle flexing. More trade, more economic help still cultivates hope for the fragile planet. If there should be war, there should be a war on poverty. Thus, the chapter presents a win-win scenario. It is critical to realize that national governments must play a critical leadership role in these activities.

References

Myrdal, Gunnar (1968), *Asian Drama*, New York: Pantheon.
Yew, Lee Kuan (2000), *From Third World to First*, New York: Harper Collins Publishers, 61.

Chapter 10
Treating the Consumers at Different Levels of the Pyramid

Although in one sense this whole book is about treating global consumers well and satisfying their needs, 21st-century capitalists will have to have a different orientation than their earlier predecessors of the 19th or 20th centuries. Much less emphasis must be put on laissez fairism, and much more emphasis on social capitalism is needed; this difference needs very serious attention. There are a number of critical reasons for this needed attitude change.

First, as discussed earlier, the world's consumers can be described in the form of a pyramid with five economic tiers. Tiers 4 and 5 are the lower end of the pyramid. These tiers are growing faster than the top of the global pyramid, and they represent the majority of the world's population (Prahalad 2005; Samli 2004).

Second, the lower tiers combined have substantially large purchasing power which is not paid much attention to, and this purchasing power is increasing rapidly.

Third, the modern capitalist of the 21st century must realize that without improving the quality of life of the lower tiers of the global pyramid, there will not be an improvement in the fragile planet and this means not necessarily a positive scenario for the modern capitalists since there is much potential business possibilities in these markets. Thus, the modern capitalist must understand that if the benefits of globalization are not shared, there may be more international terrorism.

Fourth, the modern capitalist must understand that by improving the quality of life of the pyramid from the bottom, the whole pyramid's quality of life improves. This raises the level of the whole pyramid. Everyone benefits from it.

Finally, fifth, the lower tiers of the global pyramid require somewhat different treatment than the upper tiers. Although it is profitable to cater to the lower tiers and they are growing fast, it is critical to understand the special needs of these tiers and clearly decide what to do to satisfy the prevailing needs.

Maslow's Hierarchy and the Global Pyramid

Abraham Maslow put forth a theory of hierarchy of needs in 1954 (Samli 1995). Although this particular theory has been widely accepted particularly in marketing circles in North America, it has not been extensively applied internationally. In general, however, based on Maslow's Theory, it has been generally accepted that

A.C. Samli, *Globalization from the Bottom Up*,
DOI: 10.1007/978-0-387-77098-7_10, © Springer Science+Business Media, LLC 2008

in all societies higher level needs become more dominant as lower needs are satisfied. Cultural differences and different states of economic development modify both higher and lower levels of needs and desires for products and services.

Although Maslow's hierarchy has been considered to be culture specific and strongly leaning toward American culture, it also has critical messages for 21st-century capitalists. From a social hierarchical perspective, consumer needs vary quite noticeably. Thus, creating consumer satisfaction is very closely related to understanding these different consumer needs and satisfying them effectively. Maslow proposed a five-stage hierarchy. These are basic physiological needs; safety and security needs; belongingness needs; esteem needs; and finally, self-actualization. This hierarchy model is related to the level of economic development, the culture, and the social psychology of a society. As displayed in Exhibit 10.1, the hierarchy levels, in general terms, coincide with the tiers of the global pyramid. As can be seen, the type of products that are needed and purchased by the tiers vary on the basis of the approximate location of different groups in the pyramid.

As we explore the types of products or services needed, we can see that the products or services that are associated with tiers 4 and 5 are very basic and necessary for existence. Herein lies the key for modification of capitalist orientation in the 21st century. The information presented in Exhibit 10.1 is transformed into general need levels and are presented in Exhibit 10.2.

In Exhibit 10.2 perhaps the most important aspect of understanding consumers worldwide is presented. That is, between tiers 1 and 5, the consumer orientation of the modern capitalist has to change. While in tier 5, less-developed countries need products that will satisfy physiological needs. In tier 1, global consumers will try to satisfy their meta needs that would give them self-actualization. The obvious needs in tier 5 are related to food, shelter, clothing, and, perhaps, very basic

Exhibit 10.1 Maslow's hierarchy as it is connected to needs

STAGES		PRODUCT/SERVICE NEEDS
First Tier	Self Actualization	Art, education, leisure
Second Tier	Esteem Needs	Jewels, original paintings, expensive cars
Third Tier	Belongingness Needs	Clubs, groups, networks, family
Fourth Tier	Safety and Security Needs	Medicine, radial tires, health insurance
Fifth Tier	Basic Physiological Needs	Food, shelter, clothing

Exhibit 10.2 Utilization of information, education and protection

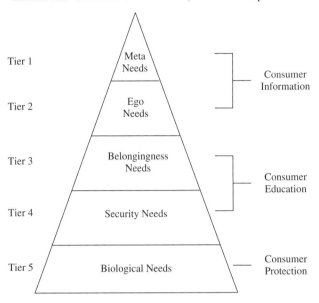

medical services in terms of vaccinations and very basic education. In tier 1, on the other hand, consumers desire art, education, and leisure. The important point is that the modern capitalist must know the difference between consumer information and consumer protection. At the tier 5 level of the global pyramid, consumers are extremely dependent on basic products and services. In that sense, they are totally helpless. They cannot quite choose or fight back when the products are deficient. In fact, if basic food items, for instance, are spoiled to the level of food poisoning, they are likely to die in extremely large numbers. Certainly this scenario is not in the best interest of the modern capitalist.

The question here is how can we help the lower fourth and fifth tier to lift themselves up to the point of self-actualization? The author believes that the modern capitalist swayed by the profit motive kindled with ambition is likely to help these groups to be lifted to the higher levels of the hierarchy put forth by Maslow. If successful, in total, this activity is likely to create more profit than the laissez fairer's gains by being only with the top two tiers.

The Modern Capitalist and World Consumers

The modern capitalists would understand that the well-being of consumers every-where, regardless of their position in the global pyramid, is their best interest. But on the basis of Maslow's hierarchy as the classification presented in Exhibit 10.2, treatment of consumers becomes different at different levels of the classification.

Although consumer information, consumer education, and consumer protection are key tenets of proper consumer treatment, and they are all needed in all tiers, these three have different weights or different importance at different levels of the hierarchy. At tiers 1 and 2, consumers are rather accomplished, well off and quite independent. Thus, the best appeal to this group by the modern capitalist is providing goods and services required at that level with special emphasis on consumer information. For those consumers in these tiers or hierarchy levels who are mainly cognizant of their needs and rather well educated, the best thing that can be done is that to provide them with detailed consumer information about the products and services so that they could make up their own minds and satisfy their own needs.

In tier 3 and the top part of tier 4, consumer education is considered important. Most of the people in these tiers are at least partially upwardly mobile, and it is critical for them to learn more about products and services so that they could make up their minds and, again, satisfy their needs.

Perhaps the most critical area in treating the consumers who are at tiers 4 and 5 is that these people are extremely vulnerable. If the products and services they are using are life threatening not only would they not know in advances but also they would not have recourse even if they knew the danger in advance. Here the modern capitalist will have to make sure that the greed factor is totally abandoned. When asbestos production in the United States was banned, the manufacturers went to India. They produced and exported the asbestos from there. This type of greedy display does more harm than good. Thus, it is critical that consumer protection is established and enforced particularly for the lowest group in the global pyramid. What are the rules of protection? How much of it can be truly enforced and how does this enforcement materialize are the questions that need to be raised and hopefully are answered.

The modern capitalist will understand that the bottom of the global pyramid is very large (Prahalad 2005), and consumers in these tiers need to be treated with more care and compassion. In return, there will be tremendous amounts of profit flowing in continuously as a reward of the efforts in satisfying consumer needs.

Summary

This chapter accentuates the fact that the global economic pyramid has multiple layers. In essence, this author maintains that the layers of the economic pyramid correspond with Maslow's hierarchy. Understanding this similarity would enable us to identify the needs of lower layers. This understanding would facilitate the bottom-up entrepreneurship. Dealing with the lower layers of the global economic pyramid necessitates informing, educating, and protecting consumers.

References

Prahalad, C. K. (2005), *The Fortune at the Bottom of the Pyramid*, Upper Saddle River, NJ: Wharton School Publishing.

Samli, A. Coskun (1995), *International Consumer Behavior*, Westport, CT: Quorum Books.

Samli, A. Coskun (2004), *Entering and Succeeding in Emerging Countries*, Mason, OH: Thomson, South-Western.

Chapter 11
A Global Ethics Stand

In Chapter 10 it is articulated that particularly the people in the lower tiers of the global economic pyramid are very susceptible to outside pressures and they have no defense mechanisms of their own. If 21st-century capitalists use their economic power to exploit the weaknesses of the people in these tiers to gain immediate economic benefits at the loss of long-term greater gains for all parties, disaster will ensue. There will be mass discontent, class wars, and deaths. Such orientation may be coined imperialism that substitutes force for freedom and does not allow healthy free markets to emerge (Paulson 2005). As Hodgson (1992) stated there is much to be accomplished and mutually gained through understanding and respect on the part of both parties and across cultural lines. One may add to this that there is also much profit opportunity to be benefited from.

Differing Opinions About Ethics

There are many different opinions about what constitutes ethical behavior. When the global scene is explored and a semblance of global ethics is considered, the issue becomes infinitely more complex.

Idealistically speaking, businesses should be concerned about something more than making money; however, in reality, without public pressures, laws, economic or business forces, there is no reason for the modern capitalist to be ethical, whatever this may mean.

But if the modern decision maker were to understand that satisfying customers is a big investment for the future, then the individual decision maker may be persuaded to act fairly and benevolently, which can be considered ethical behavior. Paulson (2005) presents an integrated perspective for international business ethics. He emphasizes following local codes and global values. In other words, local applications of global values may differ, but maximizing owner values emphasizing long-run gains will not be altered.

A.C. Samli, *Globalization from the Bottom Up*,
DOI: 10.1007/978-0-387-77098-7_11, © Springer Science+Business Media, LLC 2008

Exhibit 11.1 Ethical motivation of the modern capitalist

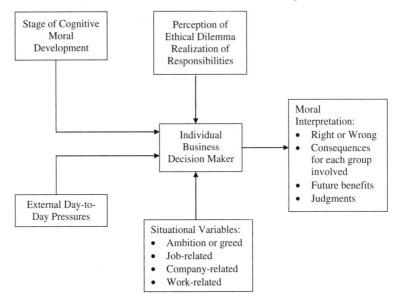

Source: Adapted and revised from Samli (1992).

Global Ethics and Modern Capitalists

Despite the constructive model put forth by Paulson (2005), the individual decision maker is likely to experience different pressures in regard to global ethical decisions. Exhibit 11.1 illustrates some of the most prominent ethical pressures that the global decision maker is likely to experience. Perhaps, above all, the decision maker, just like any other person, has a cognitive moral development stage that will screen the ethical problem and interpret it (Samli 1992). This implies that every 21st-century capitalist may perceive an ethical issue differently based on his or her background and sensitivity toward the issue or issues in question. As illustrated in Exhibit 11.1, there are two other groups of mediating variables. These are external day-to-day pressures and situational variables.

External Day-to-Day Pressures[*]

Every individual decision maker experiences immediate survival instincts as he or she is faced with a decision situation. Perhaps unfortunately, the authors believe that the survival instincts are more basic than the instincts to do good to others or ethical behavior. A rather simple example of this is the Donner Pass episode

---

[*] This section borrows from Samli (1993).

which may be considered as a black page in American history. Civilized people were trapped on a snow-covered mountain and they resorted to cannibalism for survival and ate each other. Thus, the modern global capitalist perceives a situation to be threatening his/her survival; it is quite reasonable to assume that the survival instinct will overcome the instinct to behave ethically. The threat may be from, say, some competitors or from a foreign government; however, the resultant unethical behavior can be devastating for the lower part of the global economic pyramid. Similarly, if, say, the international capitalist is facing possible bankruptcy, he or she may not take ethical behavior nearly as seriously as survival. The outcome of this orientation may mean the capitalist may resort to unethical means to survive (Samli 1993). Thus, survival instinct is a powerful mediator of global ethics behavior.

Situational Variables

Situational variables represent the environmental conditions under which decisions are made. They are different from day-to-day survival factors. Four such conditions are presented in Exhibit 11.1. The first one is more controlling than the other three. In fact, it is quite likely that it modifies the other three. If the modern capitalist is motivated by the greed factor rather than ambition as discussed in Chapters 1 and 4, then the actions will be totally short-run oriented and perhaps to the detriment of global consumers at tiers 4 and 5. It is quite possible that the greed factor makes the businessman gouge international consumers by charging high prices for low-quality merchandise. They may even sell unsafe and borderline dangerous materials or products. As was mentioned earlier, these groups of consumers do not have built-in protection and they are extremely vulnerable. Job-related, company-related, and work-related situational conditions can, individually or jointly, cause critical international damage. Someone from Enron or from an international giant can easily misguide, exploit, or endanger the consumers who are at the lower tiers of the global economic pyramid.

As job-related variables may allow a capitalist to exercise greed, company-related factors could empower the capitalist to do so. Finally, work-related factors such as the role to be played, the risk to be taken, process to be used, and so on, can reinforce that strength. Once again, as discussed throughout this book, if the fragile planet does not survive, no one benefits. Similarly, if the fragile markets do not become stronger, everyone loses. When the decision maker perceives an ethical dilemma, and there will be many of these, this perception is mediated powerfully by these situational variables. The decision maker at this point makes a moral interpretation based on what is right and what is wrong. This interpretation is based on personal thinking. Here the decision maker evaluates the consequences of the decision on each and every global market segment involved in the ethical dilemma under consideration. Finally, the decision maker reaches a judgmental phase. The individual decision maker judges the alternatives to make a decision. Here it is hoped that the decision maker, as Paulson (2005) suggests, will follow local codes and global values and would emphasize owner values and long-run gains. As illustrated in Exhibit 11.1, the outcome of this whole process is reflected in the decision maker's moral interpretation, whether the decision is right or wrong, whether the consequences of the decision can be fairly perceived, whether or not the decision maker truly calculated the future benefits and judged the whole process accordingly, which would make a tremendous difference for the future of the fragile planet.

Interferences

At least four specific conditions in modern-day global business are still influencing ethical decisions in the direction of rather poor ethical behavior. If the modern capitalist does not see the negative influence of these interfering conditions, there will be little chance for the fragile planet to have a satisfactory and progressive future. These four conditions are first, the lack of ethical values and orientations for the wholeworld; second, the survival instincts are still very powerful; third, the situational factors can be overwhelming; and fourth, short-term orientation can be overwhelming (Samli 1992). These are briefly discussed further in the reminder of this chapter.

The Lack of Ethical Values

Most decision makers, or for that matter most people around the world, do not have a background that leads to certain and broadly shared ethical values. Unfortunately, instead, there are varying backgrounds that are not shared commonly. The lack of enlightened self-interest, where one's overall well-being is intensified by the enhanced well-being of others is not practiced or even understood, is a critical problem.

Survival Instinct

As is already discussed in this chapter, in situations in which the decision maker perceives the situation as one of survival, ethical considerations take a secondary position vis-à-vis the survival considerations. Retailers, for instance, at the brink of failure may sell consumers food stuffs after their specified dates or they may sell defective or faulty merchandise that may endanger the fragile consumers' well-being.

Situational Variables

Situations influencing an ethical stance or ethics-related decisions are extremely numerous and at times are extremely complex. Such situational ethics would force the decision maker to consider every case separately. Thus, there will be little possibility to achieve consistency.

Short-Term Orientation

Short-term orientation leading to the desire for immediate gratification is perhaps the most important force leading in the direction of activating the greed factor. When short-term results become dominant, decision makers would opt for decisions that would make them or their company look good at the risk of others losing ground and getting hurt.

Since these four situations can occur time and again, it is critical to first train decision makers so that they understand the outcome of these influences. In fact, the recent development of including business ethics in business curricula is a very positive step in this direction. Second, there may be global nonprofit organizations that would insure the ill effects of not using short-term orientation on the part of the decision makers. Such positive watchdog organizations can be extremely beneficial in improving the future of the fragile planet. The modern global capitalists of the 21st century will have to have a more global ethics-related orientation that would definitely benefit them in the long run. Such an orientation has to be based on enlightened self-interest where not greed but ambition factor is the focal point. Without such an orientation it is difficult to foresee a healthy future for the fragile planet.

Summary

The ethical aspects of the 21st-century capitalism that happens to be emphasizing greed more than ambition are not quite articulated. This brief chapter raises the issue that a strong ethical stance would reduce the negative impact of the greed factor. A model is presented indicating how such an ethical stance can be developed and properly cultivated.

References

Hodgson, K. (1992), "Adapting Ethical Decisions to a Global Marketplace," *Management Review*, 81, 53–57.
Paulson, Steven K. (2005), "An Integrated Social Science Perspective on Global Business Ethics," *International Journal of Commerce and Management*, 15, 178–186.
Samli, A. Coskun (1992), *Social Responsibility in Marketing*, Westport, CT: Quorum Books.

Chapter 12
The Future Outlook

Many years ago, Bertrand Russell (1961, p. 9) had a brilliant observation. He said, "...one of the troubles of our age is that habits of thought cannot change as quickly as techniques, with the result that, as skill increases, wisdom fades." If we look at the present status of the world, these observations by Russell become more real and more frightening. The skills of producing weapons of mass destruction, for instance, have accelerated as cultural, religious, and historical dogmas remained fixed or become even more forcefully fixed. In other words, wisdom has been and is fading. If human beings become (if not already) children with very dangerous toys (or technologies), there is bound to be a doomsday. Throughout this book, we made an attempt to establish some ground rules that would improve the extremely discouraging status of the fragile planet. In terms of prioritization of the ground rules, we propose a number of considerations that need to be examined and followed carefully. These ground rules are based on the list of imminent dangers to the fragile planet. These ground rules have multiple solutions, and it is essential that each ground rule be handled with the best solution.

Much research must be devoted to these solutions by the consensus of all countries. Either the United Nations or some similar organization representing all of the countries of the world must address these ground rules. Exhibit 12.1illustrates the key threats to the future of our world. These key threats lead to the ground rules that are raised here. These ground rules would lead to the implementation of the possible solutions as they are presented in Exhibit 12.1. Without addressing these key threats and finding solutions, there can be no future for the fragile planet.

1. The issue of procreation
   As touched upon in various chapters, the world population is expanding uncontrollably. Much economic gain (if any) is offset by population increases in third world countries. If this issue cannot be resolved, sooner or later the world will reach a level of population that cannot be managed. Not only are resources such as air, water, land, metals, and the like being depleted, but the natural rate of increase in population and its impact on increasing pollution seem impossible to reverse. Perhaps family planning, contraceptives, sex education, and the like may become a serious set of issues to be pursued throughout the world in the 21st century.

A.C. Samli, *Globalization from the Bottom Up*,
DOI: 10.1007/978-0-387-77098-7_12, © Springer Science+Business Media, LLC 2008

Exhibit 12.1 The key threats to the fragile planet*

Problem Areas	Possible Solutions
• Runaway procreation offsetting ecomomic gains	• More family planning
• Totally uneven playing field in trade and development	• More emphasis on entrepreneurship and infrastructure development
• Inadequate global communications	• Development of nonpolitical global information networks
• Questionable attitudes leading to hostilities	• Improvement of global communications
• Destructive militaristic orientation	• Lesser emphasis on militarism
• Top-down globalization as extension of imperialism	• More global activity
• Prevailing greed factor instead of ambition factor	• Improvements in the 21st-century capitalism
• Uncontrolled pollution caused by militaries and industries	• More stringent global agreements
• Educational inadequacies causing global misunderstandings	• Improving global educational base
• The lack of practiced global ethics code	• Making much money by creating consumer value

* Note all of these points would enhance the opportunities for bottom-up globalization which is considered to be the key to coping with the ills of the fragile planet.

2. Evening out the playing field

The gap between haves and have-nots is not only great but widening. It is difficult to see how this gap can be narrowed or can be eliminated. In the present course, the inequalities are so significant that it sounds simply hopeless. However, as was mentioned earlier, if the industrialized world that is composed of haves can understand that the economic and industrial developments of the emerging countries of the world is simply good for all parties, then there would be less greed and more ambition. As Chapter 9 posits, if they win, we win. Here encouraging bottom-up globalization through entrepreneurship needs to be carefully explored and developed as quickly as possible.

3. Global communications

Perhaps next to the population explosion, the most critical problem that the fragile planet experiences is the lack of adequate communications worldwide. It is reasonable to posit that the main cause of the cold war and its prolongation could be traced to global misunderstandings, more than partially attributable to a lack of adequate communication. The leadership of both parties, the United States and USSR, maintained their positions by blocking some, if not much of the news. Thus, populations of the two parties kept ignorant of each other, and with this ignorance, suspicion set in. As was discussed in Chapter 1, based on this suspicion, the parties drew their lines of demarcation and put emphasis on military preparedness. It is extremely doubtful that the cold war that lasted over 40 years helped the masses, even though it created a few rich and very powerful military-related people in both societies. The lesson here is that without adequate and effective communication, hostilities and resultant militarism enter into the picture. With force, there cannot be peace and understanding. With communication, there is hope for peace and understanding.

4. Attitudes and hostilities

In the absence of better communications and understanding, special cultural pockets, religious groups, and ethnic minorities are typically persuaded to take an adversarial position to others. As discussed in Chapter 1, lack of knowledge, along with very poor economic conditions and low levels of education, create deep lines of demarcation and hostility. If these are not diffused satisfactorily, they could become very explosive. This general situation will certainly endanger the future of the fragile planet further.

In particular, different world religions have been taking adversarial positions against each other and encouraging their followers to develop such negative values. Such developments, if they continue, would create a tremendous hardship on the future of the fragile planet. If one were to study world history, one would find out that numerous wars in the history of mankind were religion based. Better communications and genuine efforts to communicate worldwide should improve this highly volatile situation by making it possible to enhance understanding of and respect for other cultures and religions.

5. Destructive militarism

By definition, militaries and militaristic orientations take hard lines. Even though militarism and militaristic tendencies are likely to be more destructive than constructive, they are valued as "macho" positions. Unfortunately, diplomacy is not commonly seen as a substitute for military might. Again, with such prevailing power reliance and displays, there is almost no future for the world. It is necessary for military forces to have a better understanding of the world.

6. Globalization is not the extension of colonialism

Globalization, as it is being practiced, along with a wonderful impact, is also creating much unnecessary hardship. Many scholars believe that, in its current form, globalization cannot be sustained. However, globalization has much to offer. Instead of a top-down globalization that may be considered an extension of centuries-old colonialism, a bottom-up globalization is proposed. Small entrepreneurial firms can transfer technologies, can partner with small local companies, and reach out to the forgotten majorities.

7. Once again the greed factor

As discussed in many places of this book, while capitalism can breed greed that often endangers the fragile planet, it can also enhance the conditions for competition and economic growth. Capitalism can easily breed ambition, leading to more competitiveness, more creativity, and more economic expansion; in short, leading to social capitalism. The key question here is just how do we convert negative greed into positive ambition. This will not happen all by itself. It is critical that the 21st-century capitalism takes this difference into consideration and educates modern capitalists in this particular direction.

8. Uncontrolled pollution

   Much of the time, polluters throughout the world are going free. They are barely held accountable to certain rules or to certain administrative bodies. They prefer the cash flow of today to the devastation of tomorrow. It is absolutely most critical that each polluter is made responsible to clean up the mess it has created. Better yet, progress should take place before an environmental mess happens. It is much more economically feasible to act environmentally responsible up front than to clean up a mess afterward. However, global giants, despite the claims contrariwise, are not motivated to change and adopt eco-friendly and socially responsible practices (Engardio 2004).

9. What about education

   In a basic sense, education could be the answer to all of these problems. But creating educational equality throughout the world is not likely to happen tomorrow or the next day. However, along with communications, education is the most important tool to create a better future for the fragile planet. Emerging countries must be given every feasible opportunity to improve education in their respective countries.

10. An ethical stance

    There is no possibility of developing globally acceptable and practiced rules in treating consumers, particularly those that are at the lower tiers of the global economic pyramid. Hence, the modern capitalist will have to practice some type of ethical code that is guided by *enlightened self-interest*. This, in practice, means making money by generating consumer value rather than exploiting consumers.

The ten points made in Exhibit 12.1 and some of the general solutions may provide the foundation for a basic blueprint as to where the world may go if there is a future for it. Perhaps the most important point that is posited in this book is that these are all macroproblems. These macroproblems cannot be resolved by the current ongoing micromanagement processes of countries, regions, and companies. Furthermore, these macroproblems cannot be resolved by governments alone. The 21st-century capitalism must be very sensitive to these issues. The points in Exhibit 12.1 provide multiple solutions at each level. Under a nongovernmental world organization and with the participation of all nations (not only G-8), there may be joint solutions. Perhaps throughout this book, an extremely critical and philosophical issue emerges. That is the relationship between the private and public sectors. If the current 21st-century capitalists do not take a very strong antigovernment stance and do cooperate with the public sector, this modern capitalism will reach out to the forgotten majority. This will be an extremely powerful move in the direction of a better world. This proposition of moving from an adversarial relationship to a cooperative relationship between the private and public sectors is necessary to expand the impact of social capitalism that is advocated throughout this book. Such a goal, however impossible it seems at this point, is totally necessary. Just allowing the fragile planet to destroy itself is not in the best interest of anybody. We need more constructive, not destructive, global cooperation. The world we will save is our very own. Just how do we propose to promote social capitalism throughout the world? The following section presents the concept of the *power troika*.

The Power Troika

Throughout this book, it is posited that a slightly modified version of current capitalism (or a milder version of laissez fairism with much more emphasis to social capitalism) is necessary for the world to function. This critical modification entails moving away from greed and encompassing ambition for further growth and development. It is also posited that there is a fine line between greed and ambition, and greed cannot be controlled by telling people how to behave. Rather it can be checked by increasing competition, by developing and enforcing antimonopoly laws, and by restricting mergers and acquisitions at certain reasonable levels. But there is no way in this book the author advocates that we should get rid of capitalism. Capitalism is the trigger at the firing line that makes things happen.

If capitalism can become a little tamer, just how would it be implemented? There are essentially three powerful carriers of capitalism throughout the world. These are globalization as it functions in its current top-down pattern, local or regional governments with the power and vision to expand infrastructures, and entrepreneurs with the ability to generate consumer value from the bottom of the global pyramid. This author coins these three power bases as the power troika.

Globalization

The first leg of the power troika is globalization. This is the most powerful tool that has emerged in the history of mankind. As mentioned at the beginning of this book as well, globalization through its four very powerful weapons—information flow, technology flow, capital flow, and know-how flow—has been expanding primarily a laissez-faire version of capitalism throughout the world (Samli 2002). Although it is bringing fame and fortune to a select few, as also discussed earlier, this situation is causing more divisiveness and disproportion in the economic well-being of many groups of people throughout the world. It certainly is not likely that the current wave of globalization activity will subside or will change its nature in the near future. Indeed, it is a very important element in the world's well-being as it stands. This powerful and almost unstoppable tool is, in fact, the reason for this book. The book simply is promoting the idea of getting the best from globalization and making sure that its negative impact can be somewhat nullified or at least partially reduced. Since economic power leads in the direction of amassing more economic power, there is only a thin line between ambition and greed, the two concepts that this book delved into throughout. This thin line cannot be stopped from being crossed over by just wishful thinking. Even though during the past decade or so there has been a deluge of ethics courses in business and philosophy classes, their impact has not been likely to stop crossing over this thin line. Stopping the crossover process will be based on positive reinforcements by local and regional governments in terms of encouraging sharing the wealth by tax breaks for hiring more people, revitalizing production facilities, starting new businesses, and the like. At the same time, the excessive and fast-accumulating economic power in the hands of a few can be balanced by generating more local entrepreneurial businesses that would cater to a lower portion of the global economic pyramid. This is particularly critical because there is much opportunity in this portion of the world's markets (Samli 2004, Prahalad 2005), and there is also much unsatisfied economic needs that are expecting to be satisfied in return for very handsome capitalistic profit potential.

Government

The second leg of the power troika is the government. No distinction is made in this book between the central government and local governments, but one point must be emphasized, that is, the cooperation between the central government and local governments. As already discussed, capitalism, the power behind all economic activity in bazaars, markets, the Internet, stores, factories, warehouses, transportation facilities, and the like, all depends on a very functional and constantly improving infrastructure. Some indirect measures on the part of the government to discourage the crossover from ambition to greed are by supporting the emergence of small entrepreneurial businesses, by enhancing the development of the infrastructure to accommodate these small firms, and by levying a reasonable but progressive income tax system encouraging research and development through support of educational institutions and other similar activities that are essential in promoting and implementing successful social capitalism.

The current trends of local and national governments losing their power because of the Darwinism on steroids nature of the current top-down globalization which is basically encouraging the crossover from ambition to greed must stop. This will encourage the globalization process within the constraints of social capitalism to reach down and benefit not only a select few but many in the fourth or fifth tiers of the global economic pyramid.

Entrepreneurship

The third leg of the capitalist support power troika is entrepreneurship. This is the least activity that is emphasized in an effort to strengthen and spread capitalism that will advance economic conditions without threatening the future of the fragile planet.

1. The top-down globalization, which is encouraging the greed factor rather than ambition, is not reaching out to the forgotten majority in the world, who are occupying tiers 4 and 5 in the global pyramid.

2. The global giants are not necessarily generating new jobs and spreading the wealth. Instead, they are amassing economic power.
3. Global giants are not necessarily supporting most important research activity that would benefit the whole world. In fact, they are not particularly known for their innovativeness.
4. Local governments, slowly but surely, under the spell of Darwinism on steroids are losing their power base and are not capable of stopping this unstoppable current.

At least the above four reasons clearly justify the emergence of an entrepreneurial class that will be flexible, efficient, and creative enough to cater to the fourth and fifth tiers of the global pyramid, to generate more local jobs, innovate how the technological advances can be localized, and hence creating a bottom-up globalization. Such a bottom-up globalization is the balancing factor for the top-down globalization. It is likely to spread the global advances in technology to local markets and local consumers within the constraints of the social capitalism. Here, unlike some social capitalists' way of thinking, it is not the social capital, although it is critical in its own right, social capitalism here is developed in the direction of making the playing field fair and balanced so that small proactive entrepreneurial companies will have an opportunity to emerge, expand, and modify the extraordinary and unfair powers of laissez-faire capitalism.

The power troika will carry out one or another version of capitalism since here the capitalistic activity is engaged in the delivery of economic well-being. The fairer it is without discouraging ambition and commensurate incentives the greater are the chances of the world to survive.

Future Areas of Research Concentration

Although all possible solutions in Exhibit 12.1 would require rigorous research, four more general research areas supersede the others. These four areas are research for population control, enhancing international understanding, developing or producing more entrepreneurs, and treating the poor more kindly.

Population Control

Unfortunately, because of the religious and political pressures, little (if anything) is being done on population control. If a country's economic gains are outstripped by its population growth, then there is almost no hope for progress.

Enhancing International Understanding

Particularly in Chapter 9, we articulated the win-win scenario. Without an all-out global communication system, such a scenario cannot become a reality. But, enhancing international understanding has a special mission. Much research is needed to determine how a nation should market itself positively so that it will gain international respect, a positive attitude by other nations, and perhaps to some degree, strong international acceptance. Research must indicate how a nation can make itself liked by other nations.

Global Entrepreneurship

At the dawn of the 21st century, we still know precious little about entrepreneurship and entrepreneurial cultures (if there is such a thing). Multinational and multicultural entrepreneurship studies are necessary if we want the people in third, fourth, and fifth tiers in the world to gain attention and have consumer values created for them to improve their quality of life.

A Kinder, Gentler Treatment of the Poor

Twenty-first-century capitalists must realize that their well-being is totally connected to the well-being of the fragile planet. Treating the lower levels of the global pyramid in a kinder, gentler way is a critical element of the well-being of the fragile planet. If the poor are given an opportunity to improve their quality of life through constructive means to be achieved by guided and hard work by definition, the 21st-century capitalists will also be better off. Thus, the whole world will be better off, and the fragile planet will become less fragile.

Summary

In discussing the future of the fragile planet, this chapter articulates the power troika. The power troika has three distinct and powerful weapons that can be used to move the world away from greed to riches. These are globalization, government, and entrepreneurship. If the power troika can move in the right direction, the fragile planet will have a future. The key activity of the power troika is to implement the following: population control, enhancing international understanding, global entrepreneurship, and a kinder gentler treatment of the poor.

References

Engardio, Pete C. (2004), "Beyond the Green Corporation," Business Week, January 29, 50–64.
Prahalad, C. K. (2005), *The Fortune at the Bottom of the Pyramid*, Upper Saddle River, NJ: Pearson Education.
Russell, Bertrand (1961), *Has Man A Future*, New York: Penguin Books.
Samli, A. Coskun (2002), *In Search of Fair, Sustainable Globalization*, Westport, CT: Quorum Books.
Samli, A. Coskun (2004), *Entering and Succeeding in Emerging Countries*, Mason, OH: Thomson, South-Western.

Chapter 13
Financing the Future

This chapter is strictly an afterthought which, however, must be considered to be extremely critical. As we discussed first, modernizing capitalism and using it as a major tool to carry both top-down and bottom-up globalization to rescue the lower layers of the global economic pyramid profitably, we must consider a financial system that, certainly, works better than the current systems that are being employed. As already articulated, without a meaningful approach to the development of the poorer parts of the world, free flow of capital combined with the greed factor have been and are likely to continue making many reckless investments that have done more harm than good. Such activities are marginalizing localities, regions, or countries (Samli 2002).

One may say that it is admirable that two major international financial organizations – International Monetary Fund (IMF) and The World Bank (The Bank) – are seriously concerned about poverty reduction throughout the world. So much so that the World Bank headquarters has built into its lobby wall the slogan, "Our dream is a world free of poverty," which is nothing but a dream as the discussion in the first three chapters of this book presented. Conditions are not getting better; they are getting worse and as long as current globalization, reflecting the greed factor, remains being: "Darwinism on steroids" (Friedman 2000), they will continue deteriorating probably to a point that may be depicted as *oblivion*. It appears that the IMF and the World Bank are not doing enough to materialize the above-mentioned dream. In fact they may be simply accelerating the deterioration process (Samli 2002). "When the profit motive starts running throughout the world unchecked, concern about poverty is transferred to the back burner" (Samli 2002, 83). In an attempt to protect their investors and investments, the IMF and the Bank impose such unbelievably rigid and unrealistic conditions on their borrowers that the economic conditions just about always get worse. When we consider 1997–1999 Asian crises which began with a currency meltdown (Isaak 2005), the same patterns also appeared in Turkey and Argentina, it should have been understood that the IMF model does not work in the realization of the dream but creates a tremendous barrier to economic development of the third world countries.

Financial support to develop a better world is everybody's business. However, the general orientation to this all-important topic is flawed. Exhibit 13.1 illustrates the need for financial support in an effort to develop a better world. Without proper

A.C. Samli, *Globalization from the Bottom Up*,
DOI: 10.1007/978-0-387-77098-7_13, © Springer Science+Business Media, LLC 2008

Exhibit 13.1 Financial support

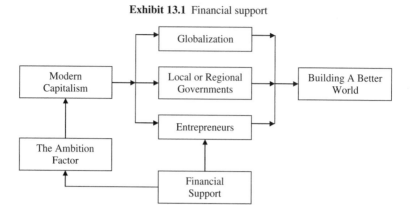

financial support, the power troika that is discussed in Chapter 12 is not likely to work. Particularly in supporting entrepreneurial activity, financial support is essential since small entrepreneurial undertakings experience serious financial deficiencies. One thing must be particularly clear, that is, the same financial model that is used by the IMF or the Bank is not simply applicable to all poor countries. This is a dramatic case of *one size does not fit all*.

Improving the World's Financial System

Financial institutions almost everywhere seem to pursue commercial and financial interests more than anything else, but leaders of these organizations genuinely believe that what they do is in the general interest of everyone (Stiglitz 2002). Indeed many believe very strongly that the whole world will benefit from trade and capital market liberalization which is the current state of affairs.

However, it is not these institutions as much as the mindsets that run them (Stiglitz 2002). Bank presidents worry about inflation statistics and not poverty statistics; the trade ministers worry about export numbers and not pollution. But unless they are concerned about the environment, about the poor having an opportunity to get out of the dramatic conditions they are in, in other words, if they are not concerned with the big picture of economic progress for all, there will be no progress.

Three key international financial organizations, The IMF, The World Bank, and The World Trade Organization, function under a particular view of economics which is not quite functional and is not likely to support what this book, as a whole, is advocating: just building a better world for all. In order to build a better world, international financial institutions are necessary but not quite in their current functioning patterns based on their peculiar market concepts.

Questionable Practices

The above-mentioned peculiar market concepts are such that they impose upon the prospective recipients of credit very rigid conditions which are likely to benefit, not the recipients, but the creditors and rich financiers in the receiving countries. The conditions that are imposed upon the prospective borrowers are analyzed here in two major categories: functional conditions and structural conditions. These are presented in Exhibit 13.2. Functional conditions deal with certain behaviors that are expected of the financial and government sectors of borrowing countries.

Here, four conditions are particularly emphasized: budget deficits, devaluation, credit limitation, and inflation.

Budget Deficits

There is a very rich literature emphasizing how, under special circumstances, budget deficits indeed could make a positive contribution to the economy. Early on the present author undertook such studies and concluded that if budget deficits are kept at a reasonable level and excess funds of the country's currency are used for major economic improvement and education-related key projects, in the long run they may pay off well (Samli 1967). Although this way of thinking may not be acceptable by the IMF and the Bank because of their unrealistic and indoctrinarian positions rather than market realities in third world countries, the author believes that a milder position by the IMF and the Bank needs to be taken if a financial foundation is laid out for the necessary economic progress in the less-developed areas of the world.

Exhibit 13.2 Basic conditions imposed upon the prospective borrowers

Functional conditions	LDCs economies
Reducing budget deficits	There will not be enough funds to develop infrastructure or other educational activity
Devaluating the currency	Increasing the earning power of foreign exporters
Reducing the level of domestic credit	Limiting opportunities for small businesses
Controlling inflation	Creating a difficult domestic business atmosphere
Structural conditions	
Freeing controlled prices	Encouraging domestic monopolies or oligopolies to charge more
Freeing interest rates	Discriminating against poorer borrowers
Reducing trade barriers	Encouraging unnecessary consumption as opposed to saving
Privatizing state enterprises	Eliminating possibilities of starting necessary industries that are nonexistent

Source: Adapted and revised from Samli (2002).

Devaluating the Currency

Devaluation of the currency for a developing country implies encouraging exports by that country. However, if the credit-receiving country does not have enough capability to export more and if it has to import some critical technologies such as information systems, energy, military supplies, or transportation equipment among others, then devaluation by definition means paying more for these and also it means earning more for the exports by the exporting country. Thus, devaluation of the currency by the credit-receiving country is hardly a reasonable proposition even though the IMF and the Bank insist on it (Samli 2002). It is this insistence that caused the Asian financial crises approximately in year 2000, the Turkish financial crises in 2001, and Argentinean financial crises in year 2002.

Reducing the Level of Domestic Credit

Reducing domestic credit expansion can hardly be a good measure if, for instance, credit expansion is used to develop educational standards, national productivity increases, or financing small entrepreneurs to create a bottom-up globalization among other possibilities, then reducing or limiting availability of credit would be detrimental for emerging countries.

Instead of such rigid rules, every case, every individual situation must be evaluated according to its merits. Different countries have different needs that must be addressed carefully, and these needs can be taken care of in different ways. Although there may not be a best way identified, there are multiple good solutions to these problems. But if countries were to be handcuffed up front with some rigid and dogmatic rules, progress cannot be expected. Limiting available credit up front is one such dogmatic rule (Samli 2002).

Controlling Inflation

In order to control inflation, the IMF and the Bank require some countries in order to borrow money and make money supply rather limited that money will not be quite readily available. Controlling inflation in the credit-receiving country may be good for the creditor; however, in the receiving country, the lack of money supply can create serious problems related to various domestic investment projects for which money is not readily available.

The Structural Conditions

The structural conditions that particularly the IMF and the Bank insist on before loaning money imply some key changes not only in practices but also in its major policies that would require some serious changes in their financial and other related structures. Four such structural conditions that are imposed upon the borrowers are identified in Exhibit 13.2. These are freeing controlled prices, freeing interest rates, reducing trade barriers, and privatizing state enterprises.

These structural conditions may create even more restrictive and rigid situations than the presently existing conditions that may not benefit the credit-receiving country. Both the IMF and the Bank have their orientation coming from Western economics and believe their current sets of dogmas are all undisputed facts of life (Samli 2002). The following discussion illustrates this .

Freeing Controlled Prices

Freeing controlled prices can be a shock to the economy of the receiving country. In some countries, freeing bread, petroleum, or energy prices, for instance, have caused riots, military coups, and other major restlessness. All older economic textbooks discuss oligopolies, which mean a few competitors controlling the market, and natural monopolies, which mean that having two or more of something will be totally dysfunctional in our society, such as two competing railroads or two sets of highways side by side are not only unnecessary but also extremely costly. Therefore oligopolies and natural monopolies need to be controlled. Freeing the controlled prices in small and less-developed economies almost automatically imply letting monopolies or oligopolies function freely. In such cases, consumer price gouging becomes a practice. Uncontrolled oligopolies or monopolies can easily take advantage of the defenseless consumers and make a very few people extremely rich (Samli 2002).

Freeing Interest Rates

Free interest rates in some less-developed economies give some major power to some of the existing banks and other lending institutions. When the interest rates are free, these institutions can discriminate against the relatively worse off consumers who do not have much bargaining power as do the rich. If the interest rates are freely manipulated, then the banks can show reason for high risk and raise interest rates for their customers who have limited economic means. The result of such practices is the widening gap between the rich and the poor, which means worsening economic conditions in the country (Samli 2002).

Reducing Trade Barriers

Reducing trade barriers is almost a given for a traditional Western economist, and the IMF and the Bank insist on it. Although elimination of trade barriers can be considered a boon for globalization and expansion of world trade, it also allows some expensive and unnecessary imports of consumer goods. Anything from chewing gum, Coca-Cola, to very expensive luxury automobiles can become a major drain on small and less-developed countries. They can cause a major drain in the much-needed, hard foreign currency that can be used in the import of high-tech industries that may become critical stimulators of the economy. While the country is in need of capital equipment and advanced technologies for its economic growth which will absorb the unemployed or the underemployed poor, spending the country's resources on some less important consumption can create a worsening situation for the poor (Samli 2002).

Privatizing State Enterprises

Privatization of state enterprises is one of the key conditions that international lenders require of prospective borrowers. A number of considerations must come to the fore in this respect. First, in an economically less-developed country, there may not be enough private capital or know-how to start certain important enterprises for economic growth. In such cases, it is critical for the government (regional or national) to step in and initiate the project, this is the only way the project will get done. Second, working for the government attracts better talent than private business. In such cultures, working for the government is a greater honor. In an effort to use the better talent in its human resource supply, it becomes necessary for the government to initiate the project. Many small undertakings have started in this manner in many emerging countries. Third, the public sector in some countries may have greater access to certain technical information, while the private sector is not privy to such technical information which is needed for the development of enterprises that are critical for that country's economic growth. Fourth, it is quite likely that there are certain gaps in the receiving economy. These gaps may represent critical needs in the country such as, say, the fertilizer industry. The private sector in the country may not have the initiative or the inclination to undertake the development of such an industry. The state enterprises become very critical to accomplish such an important undertaking. In fact, state enterprises may be the only way to develop this critical industry. Finally, many activities that are related to the infrastructure development or to support certain industries such as building roads, sewage systems, or bridges are not necessarily profitable undertakings. Therefore, the private sector may not be at all interested in being engaged in these activities. The nation's needs for public facilities and infrastructure development need to be taken care of if the country's economy and its private sector are likely to flourish. State enterprises have become a necessity so that the private sector receives the necessary support. Once state enterprises make the conditions friendly and attractive for the private sector, the country's economy blooms (Samli 2002).

It is obvious that rigid, dogmatic, and one-size-fits-all conditions by international lenders do not generate the vibrant economy that the borrowing country needs to have so that the borrowed money will have the best possible performance for the borrowing country. In fact, as seen in the above discussion, such rigid conditions may actually deter the development of the borrowing country's economy. The receiving countries are not all alike. Each has different needs and different cultural values. Forcing them to make some adjustments in their structures and functions that are not well suited to their needs and capabilities are quite dysfunctional and could make the prevailing conditions even worse. In fact, heavily indebted poor countries (HIPC), at the writing of this book, are under serious pressure to pay back the loans they borrowed. But if the borrowed money did not facilitate economic progress, meaning that the programs that were supported by the loans were not successful, the recipients are worse off.

Other Creative Solutions

The extreme capitalism that is driven by the greed factor, which has been discussed above, intentionally or unintentionally is establishing a financial imperialism in the name of global capitalism. It has been repeatedly stated that these high-handed tactics simply do not work and cause more harm than good (Samli 2002).

If globalization will continue with bottom-up entrepreneurial activity and generate consumer value for emerging countries along with the whole world, capitalism needs to be modernized. This modernization, as seen from our discussion in this chapter, must also be applied to the financial structure which is extremely lender-friendly and inflexible. Modification of the financial system is a necessary contribution if social capitalism were to work successfully.

Our discussion thus far indicates that in order for the power troika, discussed in Chapter 12, and particularly international entrepreneurship, to function effectively in implementing social capitalism, major international financiers, primarily the IMF and the Bank, must change their orientation and market it suitable for the receiving country's needs.

Even if financial results based on the conditions put forth by the lenders were to be reasonably satisfactory, these results are not sufficient in empowering the power troika. A country's economy cannot be developed by finances alone. The financial management of the country is only an instrument to implement the economic program. In this book, we advocated the development of social capitalism primarily by developing a bottom-up entrepreneurial globalization as the key solution for a better feature of the fragile planet. This means that financial support is critical but it should facilitate the economic development proactively. In other words, if the plans are made to create a new industrial sector, the funds must be available for that important activity. Just loaning the money without substantial economic plans, particularly for bottom-up globalization, is rather ineffective.

Not only financial management must administer the financial aspects of the country's economy but it should also be proactive enough to facilitate the bottom-up globalization. As Stiglitz (2002, p. 59) articulated, "it takes capital and entrepreneurship to create new firms and jobs," and he maintains that entrepreneurship is particularly lacking in third world countries due to finances. This author believes that this position is correct; however, there is also less than adequate capital.

While major international lending organizations must be urged to change their rigid and indoctrinated positions, there must also be other funding organizations that can contribute. Private international development funds that are nonprofit organizations along with individual countries' developing a funding process to support social capitalism activity are necessary (even though totally insufficient) for this goal. Individual countries here may be able to accomplish part of the financial needs by some degree and forms of *deficit financing*.

It must be reiterated with vigor that the power troika leading to the enhancement of social capitalism cannot function without powerful financial support that is proactive and free of a set of rigid dogmas. Such a system must be geared to cultivate primarily bottom-up globalization implemented by entrepreneurship.

Summary

In order to implement the power troika, funding is needed. This chapter presents a general approach to financing the future. Modern capitalism by supporting ambition factor can make a major impact. Globalization with equitable distribution systems is necessary. Local and regional governments must support entrepreneurship. Finally, for all of these activities, there must be some domestic and some international financing.

References

Friedman, Thomas (2000), *The Lexus and the Olive Tree*, New York: Anchor Books.
Isaak, Robert A. (2005), *The Globalization Gap*, Upper Saddle River, NJ: F T Prentice Hall.
Samli, A. Coskun (2002), *In Search of An Equitable, Sustainable Globalization*, Westport, CT: Quorum Books.
Samli, A. Coskun (1967), "The Impact of Governmental Deficit Financing on the Growth of Underdeveloped Countries," *Mississippi Valley Journal of Business and Economics*, Fall, 68–82.
Stiglitz, Joseph E. (2002), *Globalization and Its Discontents*, New York: W. W. Norton and Company.

Postscript

Is it necessary for global capitalism to be a zero-sum game? Could it be that it is even worse than that and those who are in power are taking much more than what they are giving, a *minus-sum* game? Why is it that the current day global capitalism does not become or is not a win-win situation?

The answer to these questions may be found in the following statement: Perhaps one of the greatest fallacies of our times is to equate democracy and capitalism. Democracy is a political concept based on one person, one vote, whereas capitalism is an economic system based on one dollar (or whatever legal tender), one vote. It has been argued that accumulation of economic power through global capitalism has been distorting the fairness of democracy. In fact, many thinkers maintain that capitalism is winning at the expense of democracy (Samli 2002). Some go as far as saying that democracy everywhere is trying to mend the ills that capitalism is generating. This means capitalism must be fairer and more caring. Hence, although it is not the title, I present the main theme of my book as *Building A Better World*. But such a development, by definition, would call for some key changes in global capitalism. I further present throughout this book *A Blueprint for Modern Capitalism*. A better world is achieved by generating a more socially fair capitalism that would not expand economic might at the expense of the forgotten majority or the people who are the bottom of the global pyramid (Prahalad 2005). In other writings I call this bottom-up (as opposed to top-down) globalization. Here, entrepreneurs from third world countries partner with entrepreneurs from other countries. They develop networks and subsequently trading blocks (Samli 2006, Samli 2004).

Exhibit P.1 sets forth the broadest parameters for social capitalism. If the economy is vibrant and the political system does not allow excessive economic power to accumulate, then social capitalism works well. This is a win-win situation. In a broad sense, if global capitalism in its current form does not create a forceful system to generate consumer value for the lower tiers of the global economic pyramid, then what is known as marginalization of weaker countries takes place. Presence of marginalization, which means the country is losing ground economically and politically, indicates the presence of a zero-sum game where economic power is gaining at the expense of weaker economies. This situation is detrimental for the future of the fragile planet that we live in.

Exhibit P.1 Movement toward social capitalism

		Economic dimension	
		Positive	Negative
Political dimension	Positive	Social capitalism. Realization of win-win scenario	Emerging nations that show potential progress
	Negative	Stagnating countries. Conditions are bound to get worse	The hopeless situation. There is no expected progress. Politically and economically a time bomb

General Characteristics of the Win-Win Scenario

The upper left quadrant of Exhibit P.1 displays the optimal position of social capitalism. There are critical questions such as what constitutes the economic dimension and how it can be determined that this dimension is in the positive zone. Similarly, questions can be raised about political dimension. How is it judged as to its being positive or negative? The author takes a more practical position. If in the current practice of globalization, participants have equal access to the benefits of the globalization process and if, instead of greed factor, the ambition factor of capitalism can be kindled throughout the world, there will be more emerging countries reaching a win-win situation. Just how would such a situation be materialized? In the broadest sense, creating more competition and generating a bottom-up rather than top-down globalization is the key force behind the possible emergence of social capitalism. In addition to the creation of competition-friendly global regulations and enforcement, bottom-up globalization generates competition that is reaching out to the forgotten majority or the people at the bottom of the global pyramid. Bottom-up globalization will not stop, but will offset the ills that top-down (or the trickle-down) globalization is creating. Generating more competition and further globalization in a bottom-up manner is enhancing the development process of a global entrepreneurial class. There are no cut-and-dried formulas for that, but international entrepreneurship is critical to reach the forgotten majority, to generate much consumer value, and to acquire much profit in the meantime. The last point here must be reiterated. By appealing to and satisfying the lower tiers of the global pyramid, 21st-century capitalists will generate large sums of profit.

However, if political conditions lead to or are sympathetic to economic power taking over the political process, then the countries stagnate. The conditions become much worse in terms of the rich getting richer and the poor getting poorer. The situation is depicted in the lower left quadrant of Exhibit P.1. In such cases, domestic class wars and international terrorism can become viable forms of expressing discontent and objecting to the unfairness of the system. Internationally, this situation will encourage terrorism and accelerate its occurrence.

If the political conditions are improving and indicating a national endorsement of what is happening, then the economic conditions can also be improved. This is the direct route to the win-win scenario. Many emerging countries are leading in this direction. The extent to which they can succeed will eliminate international terrorism and further supplement efforts to enhance global understanding. The upper right quadrant of the exhibit displays this situation. The key provision in this case is the understanding that the political system or the existing power structure would allow the presence of an even playing field and equal access to the riches of the land and educational powers of the country.

Finally, the lower right quadrant displays disaster. The situation cannot be much worse. The country or region experiencing simultaneous deterioration in its economy and its political picture is clearly being marginalized and will be in serious trouble of losing its identity and of having multiple domestic conflicts as they are inspired by class conflicts, perhaps moving to class warfare. In the recent decade, a term coined "ethnic cleansing" is the reflection of such class warfare.

Appropriateness of the Externalities

In order for countries to move from the upper right quadrant or from the lower right quadrant to the upper left quadrant, certain externalities must be present. In this book they are named as possible solutions to the key problem areas of the fragile planet. Unless the external conditions are right, it will be totally impossible to build a better world, since the remnants of 19th-century capitalism, left alone, are not likely to make the adjustments that are suggested in this book. The author truly believes that capitalism and democracy should not only coexist but produce a type of synergism that would benefit not a select few people or a select few countries, but most of the people and the countries of the world. In order to reach the goal of capitalism and democracy coexisting, the concept of social capitalism that has been posited throughout this book, at least ten key conditions must be met for social capitalism to flourish. Exhibit P.2 presents these conditions. Although throughout this book and particularly in Chapter 12 some of the key remedies are noted, it is necessary to bring these issues into focus and briefly describe them again. It must be noted that in order for these conditions to be present, both private and public sectors must work together. Thus, one of the key conditions for the 21st-century capitalism is to consider government as a partner rather than an enemy. Jointly private and public sectors can generate a powerful synergy.

Although these ten conditions are discussed throughout the book, it is critical to reiterate that the world is not growing and can handle only so many people. Decisions must be made as to how many people the earth can support comfortably and how to discourage procreation. Not only is it important that the fragile planet not be

Exhibit P.2 Necessary extraneous conditions for social capitalism

	Key points
● Stopping runaway population explosion	● The world is not growing but populations are – how far can we go?
● Evening out the international economic playing field	● Uneven playing fields lead to winner take all and corporate imperialism. They need to be leveled off
● Making global communication effective and far-reaching	● Communication and resultant information must not be a privilege. They must be made available to all
● Calming down global and national hostilities	● Calming down national and global hostilities cannot be achieved by muscle flexing. There must be soft power used by world leaders. Persuasion and reasoning is superior to muscle power
● Scaling down militaristic orientation and limiting the resources alocated to it	● Defense should not mean just military might. Understanding through communication will save the fragile planet a lot of resources
● Slowing down top-down globalization by balancing it with bottom-up globalization	● Top-down globalization unchecked is Darwinism on steroids. It will not stop and will get more powerful. It must be balanced by bottom-up globalization
● Stimulating ambition factor as greed is discouraged	● Ambition as opposed to greed is renewable and is continuing and growing. If economically powerful are made more ambitious they will provide hope and opportunity for the bottom of the global economic pyramid
● Environmentally responsible behavior must prevail	● Environmentally friendly behavior is a must, not an option. It can create more wealth and opportunities for all
● Educational inequalities must be eliminated	● Educational equality must be achieved by stopping religious, economic, and political biases
● Practicing a global code of ethics	● Practicing a global code of ethics is a must since the fragile planet needs rational and synergistic behavior on the part of political, economic, social, and religious leaders

overpopulated, but also the people must have an opportunity to improve their lives. That means evening out the playing field for all.

If there is no communication among the capitalist groups, governments, and consumers, there will be no understanding. People, groups, nations are and will be alienated. This situation will create hostility. Calming down these hostilities requires enhanced global understanding as well as visible and achievable hope for people in general and consumers in particular. If and when hostilities are calmed down, resources allocated to militarism can easily be scaled down. In fact, scaling down military expenditures is a way of calming down hostilities. Instead of top-down globalization which is imperialistic and discriminatory, bottom-up globalization that enhances competition domestically and internationally must be encouraged. This proposition goes hand in hand with providing opportunities and stimulating ambition as efforts made to discourage greed. These can be achieved by nurturing international entrepreneurship that will facilitate the advancement of the lower layers of the global economic pyramid (Samli 2006, Prahalad 2005). One additional calming practice of the greed factor is to adapt and use a global code of ethics which will put *enlightened self-interest* on the front burner.

If the physical world does not survive or is not healthy, no one can survive. It is essential that the environmental health of the fragile planet be maintained by all. Finally, almost all of the above conditions depend upon how well educational inequalities in the world are eliminated.

If these conditions are met, and bottom-up globalization along with global entrepreneurship are supported, social capitalism will emerge, and the world will be a better place for all.

References

Prahalad, C. K. (2005), *The Fortune At the Bottom of the Pyramid*, Upper Saddle River, NJ: Wharton School Publishing.

Samli, A. Coskun (2002), *In Search of An Equitable, Sustainable Globalization*, Westport, CT: Quorum Books.

Samli, A. Coskun (2004), *Entering and Succeeding in Emerging Countries*, Mason, OH: Thomson, South-Western.

Samli, A. Coskun (2006), "Needed A Second Wave of Globalization: A Vital Strategic Posture for World Entrepreneurs," *The Marketing Review*, Summer 149–162.

For Further Reading

I would like to share with you some of the recent books that helped me to formulate my thinking and my specific ideas about this book. Some of these references are footnoted in the book and there are others that are not footnoted but are equally or even more important. You judge.

The first concept is *globalization*. There are numerous books on this topic. I shall list a group of books and present a brief summary of each.

Perhaps one of the most widely read books on globalization is *Lexus and the Olive Tree* written by Thomas Friedman (2000), New York: Anchor. In a more popular and optimistic style, Friedman advocates more trade and more capitalistic orientation as a solution for the big problem of tremendously fast growing gap between the industrialized countries and the third world. He is, however, also cynical at times and labels globalization as the "Darwinism on steroids." In an attempt to strengthen his position, Friedman also came up with a more recent book called *The World Is Flat* (2005), New York: Farrar, Straus and Giroux. In this book he maintains that the world is becoming flatter in terms of ease of entering trade and conducting trade based on advancing of globalization. He presents ten reasons why the world has gotten flatter. The implication of flatness to the present is that some third world countries can develop trade with the West based on offering parts, components, semifinished products, and raw materials rather than only finished goods. This is a fine development and, of course, additional trade is better than reduced trade or no trade. Some years prior to Friedman, in a very scholarly and interesting book, Kotler, Jatusripitake, and Maesincee maintained that the countries that develop free markets perform well. The book is titled: *The Marketing of Nations* (1997), New York: The Free Press. It is also more of an advocate of privatization like Friedman. Another book along the same lines attracted my attention. From a capitalistic perspective it identifies how corporations can use globalization as a tool to gain power and enjoy extraordinary profits. Govindarajan and Gupta (2001) maintain that every industry must be considered a global industry and every business mostly functions on knowledge. Therefore every business is a knowledge business. The book is titled: *The Quest for Global Dominance*, San Francisco: Jossey-Bass, and it deals with enhancing global dominance.

Thus in the above books globalization is seen as one single most powerful economic tool to improve the economic status of all countries. However, there are others that think otherwise. In addition to my own extensive research and experiences this thinking for me was reinforced by a book by Hertz (2001), *The Silent Take Over*, New York: The Free Press, where she raises the issue of how corporations in this age of globalization are directly influencing our lives, our societies, and clearly our future. They are threatening the essence of democratic ideals and practices. This position, not totally but partially, is reinforced by the Nobel Prize winning economist Stiglitz (2002), in his book titled *Globalization and Its Discontents*, New York: W. W. Norton. He maintains that the plight of the developing nations cannot be solved if International Monetary Fund and other financial institutions put their interests on Wall Street ahead of the struggling nations of the world. By the same token, Soros maintained that the problems of the poor nations can be solved by a much different global monetary system; Soros (2000), *The Open Society*. But this whole situation of taking care of struggling countries requires more than financial solutions. In a very critical book Chus (2003) discusses that the countries that have made progress are the ones that have an intellectual elite with hands-on orientation to the economies of their respective countries. Her book is titled *World on Fire*, New York: Doubleday. This orientation can be detected in Kotler et al.'s book mentioned earlier, but it did not articulate the situation as Choa did. A very powerful book by Isaak (2005) maintains that unless the key gaps that the poor countries are suffering from are eliminated, the picture is going to get worse in the sense that the poor will get much poorer and the rich will get much richer and the world will become more and more vulnerable to international terrorism. What Isaak coined as the poverty traps – institutional, trade, education, debt, and cultural and this author added population – are discussed in this book. Isaak's book is titled the *Globalization Gap*, Upper Saddle River, New Jersey: Prentice Hall. Isaak's concerns were also articulated in one of my earlier books, Samli (2002) in which I discuss the pluses and minuses of globalization. In this book I conclude that despite all of its positive features, globalization is creating and widening a gap between haves and have-nots. My recommendation for this situation is that we should cultivate the development of an international entrepreneurship class. The book is titled: *In Search of an Equitable, Sustainable Globalization*, Westport, Connecticut: Quorum Books. In the mean time Reich (2007) articulated the set of ideas that capitalism is doing better in the world. He claims that this is due to disappearing of oligopolies. His book is titled *Super Capitalism* and published by Alfred A. Knopf-New York. However, the premise that oligopolies are disappearing is not agreed upon by this author. In my 2002 book I talked about the concentration of economic power (tendency toward oligopolization) throughout the world and unchecked this situation is becoming worse. This is why in this present book I referred to global greed which is unchecked globalization leading to global economic concentration or oligopolies. It is my contention that the current form of globalization is top-down and stimulating global greed. My remedy to this situation is stated in an earlier book and further articulated in this present book. My earlier book dealing with remedial solution to the current top-down globalization which is breeding on greed, is Samli (2004), *Entering and Succeeding in Third World Countries*, Mason, Ohio: South-Western-Thomson. In that particular book I talk about balancing the top-down globalization, again, stimulated by greed with bottom-up globalization that is driven by ambition. The ambition that is displayed by entrepreneurs is not likely to stop top-down globalization but simultaneously will start a bottom-up globalization which will hopefully stop the widening of the gap between haves and have-nots. In this current book I get into this discussion by emphasizing that capitalism is an economic system and democracy is a political system and we must understand the difference and improve our systems to develop some version of social capitalism. Social capitalism deals with rewarding those according to their contributions to the total value created rather than the winner-take-all philosophy which again is the prevalent current picture and is driven mostly by GREED. Here is, in a nutshell, my thinking and most of the key books that influenced my thinking. Make yourselves a favor and look at these books then formulate your own opinions. As Iacoca articulated in his recent book: *Earn, Learn and Return*. If you are reading this book quite likely that you are at the stage of return, please do so. We must save this fragile planet.

About the Author

Dr. A. Coskun (Josh) Samli is Research Professor of Marketing and International Business at the University of North Florida.

Dr. Samli received his bachelor's degree from Istanbul Academy of Commercial Sciences, his MBA is from the University of Detroit and his Ph.D. is from Michigan State University. As a Ford Foundation fellow, he has done post doctoral work at UCLA, The University of Chicago and as an International Business Program fellow at New York University.

In 1974–1975 he was Sears-AACSB Federal Faculty Fellow in the Office of Policy and Plans, U.S. Maritime Administration. In 1983, Dr. Samli was invited to New Zealand as the Erskine Distinguished Visiting Scholar to lecture and undertake research at Canterbury University. In 1985 Dr. Samli was a Fulbright Distinguished Lecturer in Turkey. He was selected as the Beta Gamma Sigma, L. J. Buchan Distinguished Professor for the academic year 1986–1987. He was given a research fellowship by the Center of Science Development, South Africa, February 1995. He was awarded a fellowship by the Finnish Academy of Sciences to teach a Doctoral Seminar, June, 1999.

Dr. Samli is the author or coauthor of more than 250 scholarly articles, 17 books and 30 monographs. Dr. Samli has been invited, as a distinguished scholar, to deliver papers in many parts of the world by many universities. He has lectured extensively in Europe, Eastern Europe, Middle East, Far East, Oceania, and many other parts of the world. He has been very active in the Fulbright Commission. Dr. Samli is on the review board of seven major journals. He was the first president and a research fellow of the International Society for Quality of Life Studies (ISQOLS).

Dr. Samli is a Distinguished Fellow in the Academy of Marketing Science and a past chairman of its Board of Governors. He has done some of the earlier studies on the poor, elderly, and price discrimination. His most recent books are *Social Responsibility in Marketing* (1992) published by Quorum; *International Marketing: Planning and Practice* (1993) published by McMillan; *Counterturbulence Marketing* (1993), *International Consumer Behavior* (1995), *Information Driven Marketing Decisions* (1996), *Recent Developments in Marketing QOL Research* (1996) all published by Quorum; *Marketing Globally* (1998) published by NTC; *Marketing Strategies for Success in Retailing* (1998) and *Empowering the American Consumer* (2001) published by Quorum; *Entering and Succeeding in Third World Countries*

(2004), *Up Against the Retail Giants* (2005) published by Thomson; *Chaotic Markets* (2007) published by Praeger. *Social Responsibility in Marketing,* and *Empowering the American Consumer* books were considered among the most important academic books in the United States by the Choice Magazine, which is managed by librarians. These books received the Choice award. Praeger is publishing his eighteenth book that deals with chaotic markets and survival strategies.

Dr. Samli has worked with hundreds of small- and medium-sized businesses as a consultant, over a 40-year period. Dr. Samli has given many seminars before hundreds of business managers in Turkey, Australia, Norway, New Zealand, and other parts of the world.

Dr. Samli has had more than 20,000 students from all over the world. Many of them are professors, successful businessmen, and statesmen. He reviews dissertations as the outside international expert.

Index

Printed in the United States of America